THE SILVER LINK LIBRARY OF RAILWAY MODELLING

●

CREATING THE SCENIC LANDSCAPE

THE SILVER LINK LIBRARY OF
RAILWAY MODELLING

CREATING THE SCENIC LANDSCAPE

Stations and buildings * Fields and trees, roads and rivers * Construction techniques * Painting and detailing

A series of books providing a no-nonsense step-by-step guide to model railway construction

Trevor Booth

Silver Link Publishing Ltd

First published in 1994
Reprinted 1995
Reprinted 1997
Reprinted 1998
Reprinted 1998
Reprinted 1999
Reprinted 2000
Reprinted 2001
Reprinted 2002

British Library Cataloguing in Publication Data

A catalogue record for this book is available from the British Library.

ISBN 1 85794 023 7

Silver Link Publishing Ltd
The Trundle
Ringstead Road
Great Addington
Kettering
Northants
NN14 4BW

Tel/Fax: 01536 330588
email: sales@nostalgiacollection.com
website: www.nostalgiacollection.com

Printed and bound in Great Britain

ACKNOWLEDGEMENTS

Grateful thanks are due to David Hampson, J. B. Hodgson, John Robinson and the staff at the Salford Quays Heritage Centre and Bolton Local History Library who have helped enormously by allowing me to use photographs and providing help and information.

Special mention must go to Pete Smith of Kirtley Models for help in providing the buildings, and to my wife Susan for typing and making sense of my jottings.

CONTENTS

INTRODUCTION

Left Platt Lane makes its debut at Bolton Model Railway Exhibition, giving a clear impression of what it will eventually look like. The photograph also shows how, even in mock-up form as some of them still are, the various buildings referred to individually in this volume interrelate. *W. Adams*

This, the second volume in the Silver Link Library of Railway Modelling, covers the development of what is commonly known as the scenic side of the construction of a model railway. In effect it covers a range of matters, including ballasting and painting the track, the effects that can be created through the development of rural and urban scenes, constructing model buildings, and adding vehicles and people. I am aware that I am attempting to cover a wide range of issues and hope that in doing so I have not missed out anything important. I have tried to concentrate on those areas which I believe are of greatest importance, yet without omitting completely some of the more basic matters that must be addressed.

In this introduction, if for no other reason than to explain what comes in subsequent sections and why, I will explain my approach to developing a model railway. My aim in producing a model is to please me, its builder - otherwise why do it? To please me a model railway must provide as 'holistic' a view as possible. In other words, I want the trains, their movement and the landscape in which they operate (and the manner of their operation) to convey to me a picture of a real railway operating in its environment, whether it be rural Sussex or darkest Yorkshire.

Inevitably any model must be a compromise, and if we try to deny that we delude ourselves. The modeller cannot, however carefully and fastidiously he or she models, represent weight ratios, steam, let alone animation of people and animals, smells, sounds, etc. No model can. But a model can try and give the general *feel* and *impression* of the railway in its setting and period.

The approach I adopt, therefore, is to try and achieve an overall impression rather than have exquisite detail. I liken it to impressionist painting, but with the added dimension of movement from the trains and three dimensions. Consequently my reference is to the real thing, from which I draw inspiration and which I use as a source for ideas, plans, designs and ultimately the model itself. The reasoning behind going back to reality is that it is correct in all its endless forms, and the model is my interpretation of that reality rather than that of a third-party layout plan designer or, worse still, my interpretation of someone else's model.

This impressionist or holistic approach demands equal attention to all aspects of developing the model, rather than just concentrating on the bits the modeller likes. It does seem to me a little incongruous to have beautifully detailed trains running through rudimentary scenery, but I acknowledge that each modeller brings his own ideas and aspirations to the hobby. I do think, however, that much greater pleasure is obtained from a model railway if it is developed as a whole rather than as a collection of convenient bits. I am conscious that I am dealing with intangible, rather abstract concepts here, but I hope that as the story of Platt Lane progresses, matters will become somewhat clearer. While an individual model can easily capture the character of what it represents, it only really comes alive when set in a total picture or scene - then it begins to develop an impression or atmosphere.

To some degree the scale the model is constructed in shapes how this elusive picture can be achieved. Beautiful examples of trains in the larger landscape have been developed in 2 mm scale in quite small spaces; the trains become a tiny, almost incidental part of a bigger picture. In the larger scales, 7 mm particularly, the size of the locos, stock and individual buildings, etc, is such that a different approach is needed to create the illusion in the sort of modelling space we can normally look to. I hope Platt Lane goes some way to achieving this.

Platt Lane is a conscious effort to adapt actual reality to the reality of time, space and money that the railway modeller is likely to have available. In developing the model I have really concentrated on three fundamental principles to help develop my picture:

1 Clearly establishing *where* geographically the railway is set. This gives meaning to the setting for the railway and its environment, sets the parameters for the architecture and landscape materials, and ensures the compatibility and visual believability of the separate elements that make up the model railway. So, you pick your area and study it.

2 Establishing *when* the model is set. To be effective the model must, I believe, be clearly set in a particular period. This will not only affect the trains running on the layout, but also may affect signalling and livery of railway structures, and will certainly determine the details such as signs, shops, vehicles and costumes.

3 The third essential element is inextricably linked with the previous two and relates to the choice of railway company. Each had its own style, clear and distinct, which even in today's era of electric trains still shows through between the overhead wires in terms of signal boxes and civil engineering, for example - even on the platforms. Such survivals clearly betray, say, the West Coast Main Line's LNWR past.

The town that we have used for the inspiration of Platt Lane was primarily a Lancashire & Yorkshire stronghold, but the line that Platt Lane drew on was LNWR. Accordingly, even though the layout is set nearly 40 years after the end of the LNWR, and after much cross-fertilisation, particularly of stock, locos, signs, etc, it was still necessary to go back to this origin for the basic style. Surprisingly, however, this was not the case with the main station building, which was, as far as I can gather, unique.

I believe therefore that it is necessary to try and produce an overall standard that is as even as possible and to the best of our ability. After all, it is not the number of rivets on a cabside or courses of bricks in a building that tell you where it is and give the impression - it is the sum of all the bits and pieces, some being more important than others.

I also believe that this approach lends itself to improving the standard of models for which the majority of us aim, and have the time, resources and inclination to pursue. It helps us to create our picture into which we can escape from reality - after all, isn't that what any hobby is about, escape and relaxation?

1.
THE SCENIC BASE AND BALLASTING THE TRACK

I suppose the logical place to start to breathe life and colour into the bare skeleton of the baseboard and track is with the track itself. If you take a careful look at railway track, be it on your local railway or preserved line, you will notice that there is a high level of variation in the colour, texture and general appearance depending on its usage, age and location. Two particular aspects need to be considered together, the basic ground cover and the ballasting of the track itself.

Basic ground cover

Normally the ground immediately around the track within the railway boundary has an ash or similar surface, which in itself is part and parcel of the preparation of the ground during the process of building the railway. (Clearly, other surfaces such as stone setts also abound, depending upon the purpose for which a particular piece of railway ground is to be used.) To represent the surface on a model railway is a straightforward job requiring the appropriate areas of the baseboard to be covered with a suitable ground material giving the appearance of fine ash or similar. My own personal preference is the use of a material, irrespective of the scale of the model, that is the very finest it is possible to obtain. It is worth mentioning the reason for this, which relates to the view we humans have of the model railway in relation to the scale at which we would normally perceive the real thing. A similar approach needs to be taken with the use of colour, which is discussed more fully later. Another reason for using the very finest ground cover material is to avoid it contrasting visually too much with the scale of the ballast, sleepers and adjacent vegetation. I tend to regard the general appearance given by a reasonable quality photograph as a good guide. Here you rarely find that the texture of the ground cover stands out; indeed, the impression given

is one of a comparatively smooth surface.

The ground cover material itself is applied direct to the appropriate areas of the baseboard, these areas having previously been painted with PVA wood glue diluted no more than 50/50 with water. I tend to use masking-tape to clearly define the edges of the areas that are to be treated; while it is commonly accepted that there are no straight edges in nature, we are not, in putting this surface down, dealing with a natural surface, but a surface created by man and one that abuts directly to structures or a more random and natural ground cover such as grass, weeds, etc.

I therefore apply the ground cover right to the very edges of the sleepers, to the boundaries of structures, to the edges of natural scenery such as embankments, to the foot of retaining walls, and into the 'V' angles where tracks split for sidings or between running lines. If at this stage, having applied the basic ground cover material, you get the impression that there are large areas of blackish material that don't look at all realistic, don't worry too much, as this surface really only provides a link between other different surfaces around the railway boundary to be added later.

I am a believer in taking great care and time in applying this sort of material, for no other reason than it needs to be applied flatly and evenly; it's so easy to disturb it before the glue holding it to the baseboard top is dry, and it's the devil's own job to try and get it to look smooth and even again afterwards! It is a sad fact in my experience that the slightest cough, sneeze or twitch when the glue is drying leads to pock-marks or bunching of scenic material and the possibility that other material will be attracted to the wet glue.

The principle adopted for the application of this sort of material tends to be the same basic procedure as that followed for the application of most other ground cover materials such as those that we will be using later. It is therefore worthwhile considering what is involved.

First clear the baseboard surface of all superfluous non-fixed material and brush it clean with an old broad brush to make sure there are no contaminants. Next mark out the area clearly and apply masking-tape to the boundaries as appropriate. Then apply the diluted glue as evenly as possible to the appropriate areas, followed by the scatter material. Wait for at least half a day, or preferably overnight, until this material is dry before brushing it gently with a broad, soft-bristled brush (an old paintbrush, $2^1/2$ to 3 inches wide, is ideal), trying to save as much of the loose material as possible for future use by brushing it into an empty, clean receptacle - a clean container is again important to avoid contaminants. It is surprising how easy it is to find that there is a section of wire casing or an odd piece of wood shaving that only becomes obvious when it is stuck to the area we are covering.

You will note that I have assumed that, before applying this first layer of the scenic cover, we know exactly where it is to go, and that the other structures to be placed on the railway have been marked out. This is possible only because we have, with a great degree of certainty, already established exactly the appearance we want, the contours and the location of buildings and structures, in the planning and design process, as discussed in *Baseboard Basics and Making Tracks*.

I mentioned earlier the importance of leaving this work to dry before proceeding with any further developments. I find that it is easier to work on separate baseboards independently, as often by the time work is completed on the final baseboard it is possible to start work on additional activity on the first one, the glue having dried sufficiently. One very important point concerning work carried out on baseboards independently is that exactly the same shade and colour, type and texture of material must be used. I find that you always need to use more material than you think and for what it costs it is worthwhile having an extra bag or two in stock. I will confess, however, that it is not uncommon for me to find that a modelling session will start based on the assumption that there is plenty of material in stock, only to find out that it is touch and go as to whether there is enough to finish the last square inch of cover!

Ballasting the track

Now to move on to the track itself. The first stage of breathing life into it is to actually ballast it. The work process I will be referring to and will concentrate on assumes that the track is laid first and ballasted afterwards. This process is essential in O gauge or wherever you have deep sleepers and a sufficiently 'bedded-in' effect is to be created.

In smaller gauges where very thin sleepers are used, my favourite method is to mark carefully where the track is to go, then cut and prepare it, and glue the area on which it is to be laid. Next fix the track, make any minor adjustments, then pour ballast over the track and sleepers, leaving it to dry before brushing off the surplus. This will leave the track firmly in position with the ballast glued down correctly up to the height of the sleepers. Again I use masking-tape to establish the boundary of glue and ballast, removing it afterwards.

However, back to the ballasting method used for our project layout, and indeed on all the O gauge modelling I have undertaken, where the track is already laid and wired. The ballasting method is really quite straightforward, and involves pouring appropriate ballast material over the track, brushing it into position with a soft paintbrush and applying glue to fix it in place. It all sounds very simple doesn't it? But, alas, that is not quite the case. There is a whole batch of problems that arise.

The first is the actual choice of ballast material itself. You will note that there are ballast packs advertised in the model press and available in model railway shops, purporting to be for N gauge, OO gauge, O gauge or whatever, and composed of varying materials. Dependant upon how accurate you want your model to be, you will choose the appropriate type of material and the method of ballasting to suit the area and period in which you are modelling. You can study old photographs to discover much of this information; indeed, at one time in some areas it was common for the whole of the sleeper to be ballasted over. Ash was used as ballast material in some areas, not to mention the different types of stone used in the more conventional arrangements.

Again I tend to go for the old 'what does it look like in a good black and white photograph?' method for inspiration. I also usually choose ballast intended for a smaller scale than that in which I am working. As an example, the track for the project layout was ballasted with material from the Woodland Scenics range marketed under the 'fine' label. This I would suggest tends to reflect the appearance I got from looking at photographs of railways in the area at the time. Having said that, I now look at my local railway line and at the granite or limestone chips used to ballast it, and not only has the style of ballasting changed, but the appearance of the ballast material seems to be much sharper and less rounded and settled than the older style. I've no doubt there are some people who would go to the lengths of finding out the general size of the ballast used by the railway they are modelling at the particular time they are modelling it, but for me that is going rather too far

Right This shot shows ballasting and trackwork probably as many modellers envisage it in the Steam Age - clean ballast, neat and tidy, and trackwork to match. This is not surprising, however, for this track had received extensive maintenance and ballasting a few days previously. Nice though it would be in our ordered model world, this is the exception rather than the rule.

Incidentally, the train is interesting, being a trip working from Halliwell goods sidings to Burnden Junction, hauled by a Fowler dock tank. The second, third and fourth vans behind the loco are 'Pal-vans', designed with wide openings to enable pallets to be loaded directly into the vans, thus speeding transshipment. They were briefly, from the late '50s to the '70s, quite common. *D. Hampson*

Right This shot of the approaches to Great Moor Street, the inspiration for Platt Lane, shows a rather different condition of trackwork from that in the previous picture. Taken in 1962, long after the closure of the passenger station but with adjoining goods facilities still open, the photograph is nonetheless interesting and not untypical of sidings and railways in run-down, little-used condition in an urban setting. The varying levels of trackwork and the pointwork to the sidings on the right, under the bridge, are interesting. The point rodding linking points to signal box runs beneath the signal wires to the left of the picture parallel to the track. Sketches are included later showing how this can be modelled effectively. *D. Hampson*

and doesn't quite fit in with the holistic approach that I have outlined as the basis for my approach to railway modelling.

As with the ground cover, the boundary of the ballast is delineated by masking-tape. The ballast is applied over the track and brushed carefully and painstakingly into position with a small three-quarter-inch soft-bristled paintbrush, so that the ballast chips do not lie on top of the sleepers. Be sure not to block crossing flangeways or prevent point blades from closing properly; above all ensure that the point-operating mechanisms are not impeded by the ballast. This latter point cannot be over-emphasised and may require some masking of the area in and around the point tie-

Above Another view of the outer approaches to Great Moor Street reveals more detail each time you look at it. Beside the general state of the trackwork there are the signal wires, point rodding and cranks between the rails (centre of the picture). The check-rail against the right-hand rail leading to the switch is noteworthy, as are the non-standard signal box and the subsidiary arms on the bracket - still there after the main arms have gone. The walls and masonry provide considerable variation in style and material within literally a few yards. Note the huts, not far from the signal box, and also the sleeper walkways. Who said trackwork was all the same? *D. Hampson*

Below left This is a bit more like it! The trackwork at Bolton Trinity Street in 1959, with an unidentified Fairburn tank pro-

viding the backdrop, is nearer to the appearance of that on much of the Platt Lane layout. *D. Hampson*

Below right The Steam Age railway relied on coal and water to fuel the locomotives - easily forgotten today, 25 years after the end of steam. Water troughs were not uncommon, and enabled locomotives to pick up water while on the move via a scoop lowered from the tender - the cascade of water resulting from this exercise had to be seen to be believed! This feature was obviously restricted to open lengths of line and is seldom modelled and rarely illustrated. Consequently, I have included a shot of Lostock troughs on the stretch of line between Bolton Trinity Street and Lostock Junction. *D. Hampson*

bar. Not to worry, however, as these will be disguised, providing that they are not too large, when we come to colour the whole ensemble later. It is a painstaking, boring and frustrating process to brush ballast into place and if, like me, you are on the last stretch then catch the baseboard or sneeze, you can end up having to go over the whole process again!

Once you are happy that the ballast is in place, that it has a neat edge against the sleepers, and that there are no bits of ballast where there shouldn't be, it is time to glue it in place. Running the risk of messing up all the neat work done earlier, apply PVA woodworking glue diluted with water and a touch of washing-up liquid (the latter is added to remove surface tension and help the water and glue mixture to spread and seep into the ballast and thus the baseboard underneath).

I prefer to apply the mixture using one of those cheap plastic garden hand sprays, and you will find that you need to give the ballasted track a good, even soaking. Three or four squeezes of the trigger will probably be enough to fill you with horror as the neat, carefully applied, brushed-into-place ballast starts to creep and float - but don't worry! Proceed to soak the whole area, leave it at least 24 hours to dry thoroughly, then look at it again. You will need to just flick off the bits of ballast that have now got stuck on top of the sleepers, probably using an old file or paint-scraper, then with an old screwdriver clean away the ballast that has got stuck in the crossing ways or other places where you don't want it. The whole lot will look a fairly abysmal mess until this cleaning up process is done, and you will probably find that the colour of the ballast you chose, which looked perfect for your

requirements, has also changed as well. Not to worry, we are going to paint it anyway.

When the whole lot is thoroughly dry, and before proceeding to the next stage, all surplus and loose material needs to be brushed off thoroughly and any damaged or bald patches repaired. Remove the masking-tape and carefully fill any bare edges with additional material. If there appears to be ballast that has bunched together and risen above sleeper level, it is possible to scrape this back to the level or even rub it over with coarse sandpaper. Using a paint-scraper or similar instrument, clean off any glue residue from the sleeper tops, rail sides, etc. One of the most effective implements I find for the whole process of cleaning glue off sleepers and rails and taking out unnatural lumps in the ballast is a stiff scrubbing-brush - an old nail-brush is ideal.

The next stage is to try and give the whole track and ballast an even colour base. I use a very diluted mix of track colour paint to apply a wash to the whole

Above right and right Ballast on the model, glued in place as described in the text. In the first view the masking-tape is still in place, protecting adjacent areas and providing an even edge, while the second photograph shows the finished result, with rail sides, chairs, etc, painted *Author*

track surface and ballast using an old paintbrush. I prefer to amend the colour and tone by applying several different washes over a period rather than trying to provide one thick wash. The intention is to add a certain degree of uniformity to the colour of the track - what we are trying to achieve is a little bit of evenness as a base for further colour detailing.

Once you are happy with the overall colour of your ballast, it is time to start looking at the track, picking out the detail of the sleepers and the colour of the rail. With an O gauge or larger model I paint every sleeper and every length of rail individually and the colour used is not necessarily uniform. Colour can be used to represent a wide range of conditions from an old rotten sleeper in a siding to a newly laid sleeper on the main line.

It is this stage of detail painting that really does start to bring some life and semblance of reality to the mess we had before. It is essential that the paints used in this process are matt - the more matt the effect they give, the better. I personally don't use paint as it comes from the manufacturer, but rather tend to mix and vary the colours slightly as I proceed. The basic colours are a rusty brown and mid grey, but odd touches of other colours can be mixed in periodically just to vary the tones and shades used and to take away total uniformity.

I start by painting the rail sides; a good-quality sable brush with a decent point, probably size No 4 or thereabouts, I find the most appropriate. With a little practice it is very easy to run quite quickly down a length of track on one side of a rail with a loaded brush; to do the other side I just look and touch in any areas missed around rail chairs, etc. Don't worry at this stage about covering the top of the rail surface - we will clean it off for electrical contact later. I try and use the same mix of paint to do the whole of the layout so that there is not too much colour variation at this stage. Certainly one would not want to see a clear distinction or wild variety of colour used in painting the rails; the colour should generally be about the same all the way through except where we want to create a special effect such as in a disused siding, which will be discussed later.

You don't have to wait for the paint to dry before moving on to deal with the sleepers. One added bonus of painting the rails with a reasonably sized brush as suggested is that the rust-colour paint should also cover the chairs. The area around the chair base and the sleeper itself needs now to be covered in a representative colour; my base colour for painting sleepers is a dark grey. I would also use dark grey, just a touch of rust paint and possibly also a touch of a lighter grey occasionally to represent a fading, worn, rotting bit of sleeper, and even a touch of semi-gloss black to repre-

sent oil stains or perhaps tar seeping from a sun-baked sleeper. The main impression we are trying to create is one of a dry matt colour, creating just a slight variation in shade and detail from sleeper to sleeper.

It is extremely difficult to decide the best way to tackle this process; in fact, the whole issue of talking about colour in scenic work can become rather personal. Colour and our perception of it is a very personal matter and I doubt if two people see the same shade in exactly the same way. However, the only way to be satisfied with the colours that you use is through your own personal observation. Go and have a look at whatever it is you want to colour and paint; have a look at railway track and sleepers, look at them in their different locations, in disused sidings where they are weed strewn, where the ballast has washed away leaving only the ash base, where rails have not been used for many, many years and their colour is somewhat different from those on the main running lines. The colours and effects that you see on the real thing are transferred to the model by the simple expedient of using paint - matt paint, carefully applied with regard to observation sleeper by sleeper, and avoiding spillage and transfer of ballast colour to rails or sleepers, or vice versa. Don't worry if you make a mistake - if you touch a rail or chair with sleeper colour, once it is dry you can go over it again with the rust colour. That's the beauty of paint applied thinly and carefully - if you do make a mistake, you can rectify it.

Remember also that what we are trying to create is a visual impression and you will note as you look at real railway track that there are certain aspects that jump out at you, and which really need to be recreated on the model to give it that added flavour of realism. Only very rarely do the colours jar or 'shout'; they are quite subtle in their tones and this needs to be reflected in your choice of colour and the way you apply it. You can have great fun experimenting in an attempt to re-create the effect you want - even coats with a dryish brush can add detail colours, picking out the grain in plastic moulded sleepers for example, or use greys to tone down colours to make them appear lighter. There are no hard and fast rules for painting the track - it is really down to personal preference, observation and trying to get a feel for whatever you are trying to recreate in model form.

You may wish to tone down the colour by giving the whole track a further wash with a very diluted paint mix. Indeed, there is also the possibility in some circumstances of spraying an area of track in a particular colour. In the Platt Lane project layout, for example, there is a 'kick-back' siding adjacent to one of the platforms and the intention was to try and create the impression of a seldom used, very poorly maintained bit of track. Little if any ballast was applied, then the whole thing was sprayed over with matt black paint and washed over successively to try and tone down the black and add highlights to give the impression of the rotted sleepers and little-used rail. There is no end to the effects that can be created using paint and your own observation.

Cosmetic fishplates can be added to track joints, and again if you study real railways you can see that there is a slight and subtle difference in the shading of the rust on the fishplate itself and the adjacent rail, and also often around the fishplate where grease has been applied; a very dark grey, almost black, paint can be used to represent this. Where you have sidings that are weed strewn you can also at this stage add material to reflect this. At its simplest, coarse ground cover material can be added to the sleepers and ballast, or considerable detail can be added; I have successfully used both the etched foliage available from the John Piper Scenic Range and natural dried leaves and grasses either collected while out walking or bought from florists. One particularly useful material is sold as asparagus grass; with a little colouring and additional detail it makes very effective foxgloves and other similar plants. These can be planted amongst the ballast

Right Finished trackwork fully firmly embedded in the layout. This view of Ewood Bridge shows many of the points referred to in the text about the appearance of the model, and the use of various textures and finishes to create the desired effect. The characteristic Southern rail-built signal is built from a Scale Signal Supply kit, as are the LNWR and LMS signals at Platt Lane (see pages 75ff). Ewood Bridge is based on Slinfold. *Andrew Booth*

Left Vegetation was often an integral part of lightly used track or derelict sidings. This view shows the common appearance of the ground at the ends of sidings around buffer stops, easily represented on the model by scenic materials such as coarse turf or, for the larger scales, horsehair matting with scenic scatter added for a really overgrown look.

Bringing the Halliwell shunt into Burnden Junction in the early evening in 1960 is a venerable ex-L&Y saddle tank. Many of these locomotives were converted from earlier Barton Wright goods locomotives and lasted until the early 1960s, many ending their days far from their original territory. *D. Hampson*

Just to show that I am not totally steam-biased in looking to the prototype for inspiration, I have enclosed this view of now, extinct loco and wagon types leaving Southampton. The sidings in the foreground are typical of usable but derelict track which was common until fairly recently. This is a relatively easy scene to re-create effectively using paint for base colours and weathering, and scenic material to represent the vegetation. Twists of foliage mat or, in the larger scales, dried grasses sold for floral displays can be used very effectively to represent larger plants. *D. G. Isaacs*

after detailing with paint and dabs of colour to represent flowers, variations in leaves and the like. You can also add additional ballast to represent the ballast heaps often found around buffer stops and ends of sidings, etc.

We will look at adding some further detail later, but I think it is now appropriate to move away from the track for the time being and look at some of the other aspects of scenic modelling. Before doing so, however, it is worth remembering that actual materials and methods used will vary slightly from scale to scale. For example, in 4 mm scale you can purchase track with phosphor-bronze rail, which does not necessarily require the painting of the rail sides. In the smaller scales I would not recommend anyone but a masochist to try and paint a layout full of individual sleepers, but merely in particular areas to pick out certain ones or certain lengths of track to help create the effect, for example of derelict sidings. In these smaller scales it is usually sufficient to rely upon the ballast, the wash of track colour and the painting of the rail sides and sleepers for special effects to give the impression.

2.
DEVELOPING THE LANDSCAPE

In this section we'll take a look at how we develop the landscape - the 'soft landscape' being, I believe, the current terminology.

You will, of course, have planned out how your landscape is to look and will have made the necessary provision for it to flow across your bit of country

Below To give height to roadways, for example, simple wooden blocks and a plywood road-bed can be added and groundwork built up around, as in the first drawing.

The second shows how streams and shallow rivers can be formed by creating a depression and filling this with casting resin, varnish, etc (see page 27). Ensure that the 'water' cannot escape before it sets!

Deeper water needs a different approach. Clear plastic sheet is used as the water surface, the gap beneath being detailed with rocks, weeds, etc. Paint the bed and underside of the plastic to achieve the desired effect. Special effects and further detail can be added on top, and don't forget to create convincing water-edge detail. Again, see page 27.

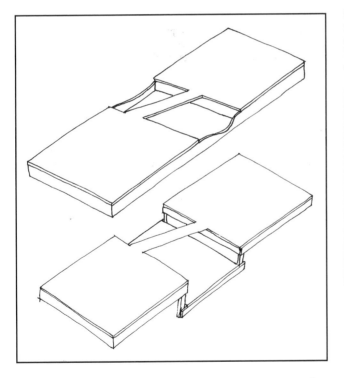

Above Even if you didn't plan your baseboards to accommodate the scenic developments, it is still possible - just - to leave the 'flat earth'. Here are two methods of giving depth to solid-top baseboards. The first shows a simple cut-out of the frame and top with a sheet fixed beneath the framework to act as a base for low-level scenic work.

The second is a more drastic attempt to add greater depth by creating a softwood subframe. It is clearly easier to work out the scenic requirements first, then design the baseboards around what you want to portray, than to adopt a solution such as this afterwards.

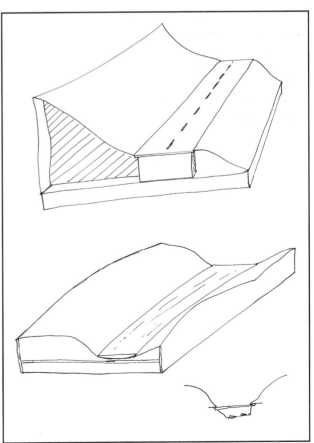

when you designed the layout, won't you? Well, you should have done, because although careful planning delays the day when you can start work on the scenery and run the trains, it makes this stage a lot easier and helps to create the illusion of realism and believability that we are aiming for.

The details of how to plan and design for scenic treatment run parallel with working out the track plan, and designing the layout is covered in full in *Baseboard Basics and Making Tracks*. If you didn't provide for the scenic development in your layout design, you won't be able to exploit the possibilities to the full, and some of the tasks and effects will be more difficult to create than they ought to have been. However, all is not lost, and the sketches on page 15 show what can be done to create depth and height after the main baseboard has been constructed.

The key thing to remember is that the landscape was there before the railway. The railway will have been required to curve, incline and develop major earthworks to fit into the landscape, rather than the landscape being built to accommodate the railway.

This is a subtle point, but one which is the key to effective and convincing scenic development. Even if your model has an urban setting, the natural landscape will have set the levels, curvature, etc, of the railway. The buildings more often than not will then have followed the railway, and may well owe their design, location, shape and function to the railway. The material of which they are built and its colour may well, however, relate to locally occurring stone and sand, more of which later when we take a look at buildings and structures.

Forming the contours

If you planned and *designed* your layout thoroughly, the base for your scenic development - the supports for the contours - will largely be in place. The first task is to fill in the gaps between them and to put down the foundations for roads, rivers, canals, etc, which it was not possible to cover during the baseboard construction.

For expanses of landscape a very useful material is expanded polystyrene - preferably in large blocks, perhaps left over from protective packing, rather than ceiling tiles (although I have never used the latter). A visit to an electrical store will usually provide a good

Left A row of small workshops typical of many to be found tucked away in the most unlikely corners, their shape often dictated by a road/railway intersection. The brick structure is clearly not rectangular in plan and has been developed to fit the site available, a process that can be replicated on models.

Below the railway, viaduct arches are often enclosed with timber, brick or corrugated sheet to provide small business premises. One unusual building still standing adjacent to the Great Moor Street route was a wooden billiard hall. *D. Hampson*

Left This unusual view near Bacup shows Pennine houses backed up against a retaining wall below a disused railway trackbed on a shallow hillside. Note how little space there is between the houses' rear walls and the 'privy'. The slope and profile of the cutting to the right and the embankment to the left are both governed by the topography and geology through which the route was hewn. *D. Hampson*

supply of discarded packing which can be used. Another source is the large blocks sold for insulation material in the building trade.

This material is light, cheap (very cheap if free!), easily glued in place and easy to work. Its biggest drawback, indeed the only drawback I can find, is that it is very messy if you have to cut it with a knife or saw - the resultant beads of polystyrene get everywhere, and because of static or whatever they seem to stick wherever and whenever you don't want them. The more you brush them away the more they seem to develop a life of their own and fly somewhere else, and just when you think you've got rid of the last bead, get out the paint or scenic dressing and another will appear right in the middle of where you are working! However, this is a small price to pay for such a versatile material. An alternative method of cutting polystyrene is to use a hot wire - see the accompanying diagram - but I accept no responsibility for this do-it-yourself device if you breathe in hot polystyrene fumes or set the place on fire! A photograph is included showing part of a layout built using this material.

More traditional methods of scenic construction rely on either a fine chicken wire or a lattice of thin card. Over these a plaster (usually using ordinary

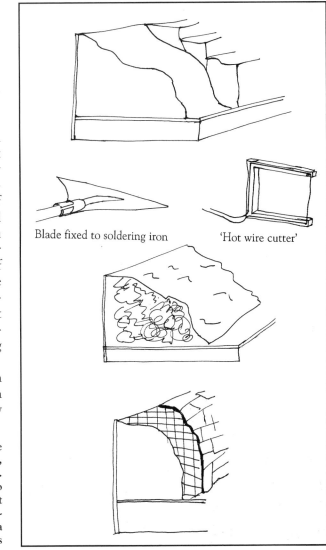

Blade fixed to soldering iron   'Hot wire cutter'

Right Three sketches showing the basics of scenic landscape formation. In the first, polystyrene packing material is used, fixed roughly into shape then carved to its final contours. This can be messy if done 'dry'. One alternative method is to attach a brass blade to your soldering iron and use the heat generated to cut the polystyrene; another is to stretch resistance wire across a simple wooden frame and connect it to a 16-volt ac supply. The wire at the open end of the frame is used to cut the polystyrene - but be careful not to ignite it or breathe in the fumes. If in any doubt, this method is best avoided!

In the middle drawing crumpled newspaper is used as the support for a plaster bandage. The effect is, however, lumpy and inflexible, and not really suitable for serious scenic modelling.

Finally we see chicken wire stretched across wooden formers, then covered with plaster bandage or papier-mâché. This is a traditional method that still has its followers.

Right Chunks of polystyrene roughly shaped to form a cutting side before being covered by a plaster surface. Note the bubbles of polystyrene all over the baseboard! *Author*

domestic filler) or papier-mâché surface is laid, forming the ground. The disadvantage for me is that the wire netting, while remaining quite still and requiring minimum support, does require pinning to the substructure and is not always the easiest material to form into the exact detail shapes and contours you want. There is also a tendency for the mesh to show through the surface unless a particularly thick cover is used; you are almost compelled to use the old plaster bandage applied in several layers to overcome this. This then becomes messy, expensive, heavy and above all prone to chipping and cracking with resultant 'white spot' - a dreaded disease for railway modelling landscape gardens (a bit like black spot on your roses!). The addition of a little PVA wood glue to the filler mix helps a little with this cracking and chipping, particularly if large areas are involved. The problem of the 'white spot' areas can also be helped by adding a little colour to the mix so that if the plaster does get damaged it won't show so blatantly.

If you do add colour to the mix, water-based powder paint of the type sold for young children is ideal, and

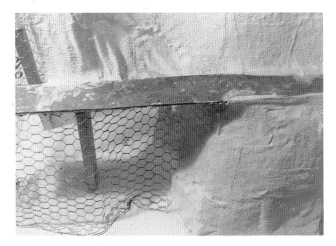

you can mix the colours to suit your requirements. However, you will need to decide clearly on the effect you want to create before adding the colour. If, for example, your filler mix is to be used as the base for the earth on your landscape, you will need to colour it quite deeply to suit the colour of the earth in the area you are modelling. Earth or soil is not a universal brown, and its colour will have an effect on the overall colouring of the scene when you add the vegetation later. There's more about creating earth and soil on page 29.

Another method I used with some success to overcome the cracking and chipping qualities of plaster alas did nothing to reduce weight or cost. This was the use of an old blanket coated in a mixture of old emulsion and wood glue, and held on to the frame with contact adhesive at the edges. The emulsion was dyed with water colour powder to a dark earthy colour which, when dry, was roughed up with a wire brush and sprayed various shades of green to represent grass, to which further detail was added as appropriate with various scatter materials. It was reasonably effective.

The lattice of card strips is just time-consuming, not particularly strong and in my experience never quite as easy as the old books and modelling articles of the 1950s would have you believe. Mind you, I suppose the blessing for the mother of the reader of the *Boy's Own Wonder Book of Railway Modelling* or whatever was that it kept the reader occupied if not a little sticky! I have a similar objection to papier-mâché, which is, in addition to being time-consuming, rather messy - at least it is when I use it.

During all these processes it is important to protect the trackwork and ballast from spillage and contamination from the other scenic effects. The simple way is to cover it with old cloth or a newspaper which can

Above left and left Scenic contours were traditionally infilled with chicken wire coated in plaster bandage or similar. This diorama shows a typical example - crude but relatively effective. The completed scene with the bridge in place still awaits painting and detailing with loose rock falls and vegetation. *Author*

either be held in place with masking-tape or simply weighted down. A bit of time spent on precautions will save a lot of heartache later.

Rock faces and cuttings

Once you have the landscape sketched in it is time to consider the detail of the surfaces. Here again a bit of thought as to what nature creates first can help produce the required effect in model form. For example, the rocks and sub-soil material were there before the grass and vegetation. Accordingly, if you have rocks and bare earth or outcrops such as cutting sides follow the same sequence on the model.

Here my method is to apply a stiff mix of household or decorator's filler to which a touch of PVA wood

glue has been added; this helps the filler to stick to the scenic base and helps to prevent cracks. The best way to prevent cracks is to build up the necessary thickness with additional layers applied after earlier layers have dried, rather than applying the filler in one great dollop. When the material is almost dry you should sculpt it to represent the type of rock or subsoil that you are modelling.

Every cutting has its angled sides constructed according to the ground from which it has been hewn. For example, the angle of a granite cutting side can be almost vertical, whereas one constructed in less stable ground would require a shallow angle. As far as the appearance is concerned, both the texture and the colour will also depend on this. It is important therefore to study - well, at least look at - the ground in the area you are modelling, which will, if

Above right and right The geology of an area will affect the contours of the landscape and the angle of railway cuttings. These photographs show how this can vary along the same stretch of line, in this case the former GWR route along the South Devon coastline. *Author's collection*

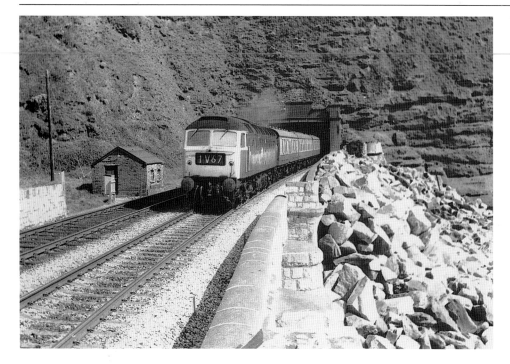

Further along the South Devon line, the sandstone rock strata is clearly seen as the railway tunnels into the cliffs. This is very characteristic of the area and illustrates how much care is needed in representing rock strata. The boulders piled against the seawall would be an interesting modelling challenge and the strictly functional tunnel would provide a minimum, literally 'hole in the wall' transition between railway and fiddle yard. *Author's collection*

represented on the model, help to create the sense of place and the total picture we are trying to create. Remember the holistic approach we talked about at the beginning of this volume - it is the sum of the little bits that must be compatible and cogent if the picture is to work. Back to 'impressionism' again.

A glaringly obvious example would be the red sandstone of the South Devon cliffs and its totally different appearance, let alone colour, to, say, the chalk cliffs of Kent. You should be able to tell one from the other without colour - just think of the impression of each in a black and white photograph, since they form the background to many a railway album shot. Each is instantly distinguishable not by colour - after all, it is only a black and white image - but by shape and texture. I suppose this is rather a long-winded way of saying that a model purporting to be set in South Devon will not look right if the cutting side through which the railway runs looks like chalk cliffs.

The way to achieve this finish is as always to look at the real thing and copy the impression it gives you on the model. You do this by carving and moulding the wet filler as it begins to set. I have found that an old table knife is ideal for drawing across the wet surface to represent the rock strata - a palette knife or similar would also do. Indeed, rock outcrops and quite a few different effects can be achieved using this simple implement. It is possible to add further effects by stippling with a paint brush and drawing a stiff brush lengthways across the surface. You can, within reason, re-carve the filler to rectify any mistakes. It is very important to make sure that the carving is consistent across the area; lines of rock strata should not suddenly change direction, for example between sections of baseboard, in an unnatural way.

If you are representing large areas of rock face or want to create a very detailed effect - perhaps the red sandstone South Devon cliffs mentioned earlier - there are other ways of proceeding. One that is particularly useful if you need to create a rock face with very little space behind it for any landscape is to mould the rock face separately; quite large lengths of rock face can be added section by section, and this method lends itself well to the provision of a backscene.

The main requirements are a simple timber-framed mould, some old newspaper and some kitchen foil; the sketches overleaf should be self-explanatory. You can of course make moulds to a standard size, and cut bits out later with a coping saw to match the contours you need. Once the moulding is dry it can easily be glued in place on the layout with contact adhesive and any gaps at the base or at the joints between sections filled with the same filler.

You can score, carve, break off or even add further pieces of 'rock', and also vary the depths and effects by deepening the mould, although I reckon about 1 to $1^1/2$ inches at the bottom is sufficient - the deeper the mould the heavier the casting. The addition of surgical gauze or fine nylon netting sold by dressmakers for hat veils pressed into the mix adds to the strength. Normally a section is about 14 to 18 inches long by $1^1/2$ inches deep maximum. You will need a lot more filler than you think! The cast rock faces can also be deliberately broken up and pieces added to other parts of the layout to represent rock outcrops when bedded in to the surrounding landscape.

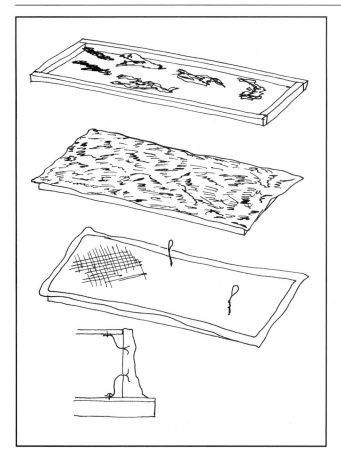

Above Casting rock faces. First make a wooden frame and place scraps of screwed-up newspaper inside. Then crumple some baking-foil, open it out and press it into the frame. Pour in a mix of filler, adding nylon net or similar to give strength. Pieces of twisted wire, their ends formed into loops, can be stuck into the wet filler. Remove the casting when dry and use the wire loops to fix the rock face in place on the baseboard.

With the basic rock in place, you can consider adding detail. Invariably any rock face will have at its foot the debris of rock falls and areas where water runs down it with the attendant discolouring of the rock and possibly algae and other growth.

Once again, go back to the source - look at some photographs of the area you are modelling and the effects you are trying to create. Don't rely on luck or copying someone else's model - they may not have got it right, and you can probably improve on it anyway, can't you?

I prefer to colour the rock surfaces as part of the detailing process later. I do, however, like to add a touch of colour to the mix, but not one so deep that it makes it difficult to create detail effects with later colour washes. Indeed, for some types of rock face, such as the chalk cliffs mentioned earlier, the merest hint of grey or yellow to just take the edge of the whiteness of the filler is all that is required. After all, you don't want to have to paint them white later!

The application of washes of paint is recommended, building up the type of colour and finish you want. Let the colour run and blend, add additional washes or changes in shade for effects and let the wash run into the nicks and crevices. I prefer to use water-based paint - cheap water colours of the tube variety or the large pallets sold as children's paint sets are ideal, as is a broad brush.

One advantage of using filler mixes that have some colouring added is that you can break up dried lumps of the stuff, even crush it back to a power, to represent the fine rocks and debris at the bottom of a rock face or in depressions. This can be glued into place with PVA glue.

Left Rock cutting (left) and retaining wall (right) on the approach to Sough Tunnel on the Blackburn to Manchester line. Because of the hard rock the side of the cutting could be steep, something not possible in a cutting in softer, less stable material. *D. Hampson*

Note in this view of the southern approach to Sough Tunnel after the landslide of 1964 how stone water courses have been constructed to take water from the surrounding land. These are the sort of details you need to be aware of when planning your model. *D. Hampson*

The addition of vegetation is simply achieved by adding various scenic dressings on ledges or at the base of cliffs, etc. Small bushes growing out of crevices can easily be represented by tufts of the tree foliage mats such as those in the Woodland Scenics range, and in the large scales by the use of detailed small bushes and trees sold as such for use in the smaller scales. Algae is probably best represented by paint judiciously applied and toned into the overall effect. Water runs can easily be represented by gloss varnish; where, for example, the water has brought out ironstone deposits and discolouring, the varnish can be applied over appropriate colouring of the rock.

In this instance, as with the other 'highlight' effects achieved with paint, it is usually better if the colouring is applied by the 'dry brush' technique. Effectively this requires paint to be wiped from the brush on the edge of the palette; the resultant empty, almost dry, brush still has some paint in it which, when the brush is rubbed over the model, leaves a sparing deposit of the colour.

Roads and water

Before returning to the general landscape and representing the various types of vegetation and ground cover, there are one or two other special circumstances such as roads and waterways that should ideally be catered for when planning the layout and designing the baseboard. If this has been done you will in all probability have provided the base on which to develop these features; ideally $^1/_8$ in (4 mm) plywood should form a good base on which to work. The meanderings

of rivers and roads can easily be catered for by using a jigsaw to cut the plywood to the shape you require.

Generally speaking I tend to model roadways, major rivers and canals somewhat under scale width, otherwise they can tend to dominate the landscape and have a greater visual impact than is desirable. This idea of modelling scenic features, particularly buildings, under scale is something to which we will return later, but is I think partly necessary as a result of the different levels and views we have between reality and the model. If you get the chance to take one of those helicopter trips often offered at summer events it is worth it if only to see how 'model-like' reality is when viewed from a great height, and indeed how well realistic models represent the view from on high!

If we look firstly at roadways, these can be categorised broadly into three types: stone setts/cobbles, stone/earth, and concrete/tarmac. In the Platt Lane project layout the roads were easy to cater for in the baseboard design; indeed, the surface was in many instances an integral part of the baseboard construction, so they had a good solid base on which to develop some detail.

The Platt Lane roadways are principally of stone setts. It is a popular myth that this type of roadway construction is 'cobbled'. While undoubtedly there were roads made of cobbles, the type most people think of as being cobbled are in fact made of stone setts.

Traditionally the way to construct model roadways of this type was to carve laboriously the effect from filler or similar material spread across the appropriate area of baseboard. Thankfully, however, embossed and moulded plastic sheets have now become readily available to suit the popular modelling scales. The Platt Lane project layout is O gauge, 7 mm/ft, 1:43 scale, and the material used for the stone setts is Wills moulded stone setts intended for 4 mm/ft, 1:76 scale! As I mentioned earlier, this theme of using materials intended for smaller scales will recur, particularly when we are considering the use of materials for O gauge.

Photographs throughout the book show how the sheets of setts have been fixed to the baseboard. Despite its drastic effect on plastics, I have fixed it in place with contact adhesive; provided that you do not overdo the application, the Wills material seems in my experience to be thick enough not to be adversely affected by it. The adhesive is spread on to the base-board surface only and, when it starts to become tacky, the sheets of stone setts are pressed into place.

Whole sheets are applied first, then any gaps or small areas cut and filled later. Cover just enough baseboard with adhesive for a few full sheets at a time rather than covering the whole area in one go - unless of course you only have a small area to cover!

If you have a look at any large area that is surfaced

Right and above right These photographs show roads made from stone setts, and the bridge one also shows a stone flag pavement. When modelling this type of roadway, proprietary scenic sheets can be used effectively. *D. Hampson*

in setts you will see that very often these have lines of larger stones at different angles to the main rows of setts. These stones are similar to those that you see adjacent to the kerb in a roadway, and I believe that their purpose is partly to hold in place the stone setts, acting as a sort of frame. The Wills sheets incorporate these stones along their edges; clearly they will need to be trimmed off as the sheets are joined. In order to get them to butt together in anything like a satisfactory way, avoiding unsightly gaps, the edges should be chamfered from the back. Incidentally, I find the easiest way of cutting these sheets is to score them repeatedly with a sharp craft knife from the top surface. The plastic from which they are made does not lend itself to the usual score-and-break technique used with plasticard; it is not the easiest of materials to work nor the cheapest, but does, I believe, give good results with far less effort than carving individual setts or sticking on bricks one by one.

Being basically lazy, I used the necessity of incorporating the framing stones around the setts to my advantage when covering the yard area near the coal drops, and avoided having to cut off all the edges and chamfer them. However, there is a different situation on the roadway where the large stones occur at the gutter and where there is a need to represent the camber of the road itself. This is easily done by using strips of plasticard (cardboard would also suffice) in the centre of the roadway, glued down to the base on which the sheet of setts is later itself fixed. If you are modelling in 4 mm scale and your roadway is only the width of a single sheet, you will find it necessary to pre-bend the sheet between your fingers prior to fixing it into place. Where the width of the roadway requires more than one sheet, it is useful, if possible, to arrange the joint along the centre line of the carriageway to take advantage of the pre-fixed strip in helping to make a sufficiently sturdy joint.

There may well be the inevitable small gaps and irregularities, particularly where small pieces have been patched in to fill irregular gaps. In this case carefully sand the joint and with an old brush or the end of the finger smooth in some filler, ensuring that you wipe it away from the surrounding area to avoid damaging neighbouring details. Detail can be added by cutting out squares and shapes for grids and manhole covers, etc, which are available as detail etchings for most of the popular modelling scales.

The key thing, apart from obvious care and neatness, in laying these sheets is to ensure that the rows of setts and their alignment is consistent. It is the easiest thing in the world to find an odd bit that will fill a small gap, only to realise when the glue is dry or you are ready to paint it that the stone course lies in the

wrong direction to the neighbouring area - I know, I've done it!

Similarly, care is needed when roads meet at intersections to ensure the correct pattern in the laying of the setts. Having said that, I'm not sure that a standard exists, as I have seen several variations, some involving the larger framing stones, some not.

Painting the setts really brings them to life and, as with the rock faces we discussed a moment ago, thin washes of appropriate colour are the best way, with a little dry brushing to add highlights. Enamel or acrylic paints can be used, but you must ensure a dead matt finish unless you wish to represent a wet surface. I still prefer good old enamel paint, and there are a wide range of browns and greys in the military colours that can form a useful base from which to start. After you have applied the washes, you can begin to represent detail such as highlighting wear, marks from tyres, coal dust in the yard, etc.

The next type of road surface to consider is the stone or earth 'dirt-track'. Whilst these are often associated as being peculiar to the rural scene, they were not uncommon in the urban setting. Indeed, even today many back streets and roads to factories are unmade, owing their origins to a cinder covering of packed earth. Today they are more likely to be full of pot-holes filled with anything from old bricks and railway sleepers to road scrapings - now there's a modelling challenge!

Roadways surfaced with stone chippings or shale were not uncommon as station approaches in rural areas. Again, it is a question of building from a solid base, coating this with glue or a matt enamel or emulsion and applying an appropriately coloured fine coating of suitable material.

I have in the smaller scales used Woodland Scenics fine turf mixture of the earth varieties, and in the larger scales, particularly O gauge, the very fine ballast that firm also produces; it is also available in a wide range of colours. You can, of course, apply a suitable material and paint it according to your choice - again thin washes are used to build up the desired effect and details can be added to hint at use and abuse. This is probably the simplest type of surface to represent, but nonetheless one that requires care in the selection of materials and their use. Don't forget grids, manhole covers and in some cases stone gutters.

Packed earth is a different matter and there are two basic ways of dealing with this - pre-coloured filler brushed on to the base can have wheel ruts, pot-holes and the like added when almost dry, or a bit of variety can be created by stippling the damp filler and adding scenic scatter material. As with the rock face considered earlier, the colour mixed with any filler should not be too dense - further details and effects can be

This rough track surfaced with stone chippings gives a good indication of the appearance of this finish. Note also the grass between the wheel tracks and the lush vegetation beneath the fence - tracks like this are commonly modelled but often present too clinical an appearance. *Author*

while the paint is still wet. You can either paint it afterwards, which you should do anyway to get the best effect you can, or hope the powder absorbs the dark wet paint (charcoal or dark grey gives a good base) and gives you the desired effect.

Fine abrasive papers of varying textures and indeed colours can be bought, and one can usually be found that is suitable for most uses. I find the biggest drawback is actually piecing the sheets together without leaving an unsightly joint when a large area is being covered. This seems to be hardest to disguise with wet-and-dry paper, which also seems to be marked very easily; anything that comes in contact with it seems to leave a deposit behind in the abrasive material.

Despite these commonly used methods of representing tarmac roadways, to my eye, using the old photograph test, this type of road surface seems to be smooth in appearance. Accordingly I think if you are trying to represent tarmac by one of these methods, the very finest powder dusting or abrasive sheet should be used. Indeed, providing no wood-grain can be seen through from the base, a painted hardboard or plywood surface, carefully executed and with the appropriate use of colour - definitely not black, please! - can be as effective as anything, and it certainly makes the painting of road markings a sight easier! Once again, as with setts, whatever colours

added with the paint brush. You can also add brick (bits of embossed sheet) and old railway sleepers to show where the roadway has been patched by pressing them into the wet plaster to achieve your desired 'repair' effect - even ballast to represent roadstone can be added.

Tarmac can be represented in a variety of ways. One method is to sprinkle fine powder (talcum powder, for example) through a sieve on to a pre-painted surface

A packed earth road surface in a scrapyard - note the wheel ruts worn smooth and the marks left by heavy objects being dropped or dragged.

This small scrapyard could be easily reproduced using scrap materials, spare components from kits, etc, and such facilities were common neighbours to railways. When looking to fill odd spaces around a model railway layout, it is surprisingly easy to find inspiration such as this from reality. *D. Hampson*

Reference is made in the text to the use of photographs as a guide to what things *actually* look like. Here it can be seen that a tarmac road surface is quite smooth in appearance, and is thus best represented by the very finest powder dusting or abrasive sheet. *Author's collection*

and paints you use in your roadways, always use dead matt - unless you want to create a rainy-day scene, of course!

Pavements are a feature seldom modelled with any degree of care, and yet so often go with roadways. I cannot believe the number of model townscapes that have pavement and roadways at the same level or are represented with just a strip of card or printed paper.

Moving on to waterways, again a good solid base is required and there is infinite scope for adding a bit of waterway to almost any layout.

If we start with a river or stream, I prefer to have a plywood base on which to develop the watercourse, as with the roadway. This should follow the course of

Pavements should be proud of the roadway. To do this it is necessary to pack them on pieces of plasticard to achieve the correct effect, as shown here. *Author*

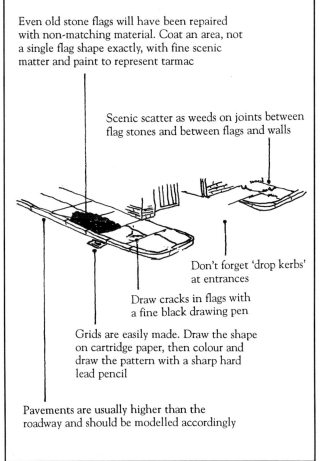

Even old stone flags will have been repaired with non-matching material. Coat an area, not a single flag shape exactly, with fine scenic matter and paint to represent tarmac

Scenic scatter as weeds on joints between flag stones and between flags and walls

Don't forget 'drop kerbs' at entrances

Draw cracks in flags with a fine black drawing pen

Grids are easily made. Draw the shape on cartridge paper, then colour and draw the pattern with a sharp hard lead pencil

Pavements are usually higher than the roadway and should be modelled accordingly

Detailing pavements

your river or stream, be a little wider than the intended width of the finished water, and be firmly in place before you begin to think about the water. When you have the base in place, it is necessary to add the boundaries of the 'water' because you will invariably represent it with a substance that is poured into place. You need to ensure that any of the liquid cannot escape its intended resting place and either contaminate other neighbouring ground or spill out on to the floor. Not only is this messy, but it is also wasteful; despite protestations to the contrary from those who are supposed to know, the rate of inflation on the products we use makes unnecessary wastage too expensive a luxury.

In effect you are creating the depression in which the water flows. For a small stream this need only be shallow, while a fast-flowing river will require rather more depth, as will a pond. Mill races and canals are a different matter altogether, and we will have a look at them in a moment. You also have to prepare the river or pond bed and plan for any vegetation that will grow out of the water.

Lest you have any thoughts about using real water, let me say that it seldom looks effective on a model, is hardly a realistic proposition for anything but a permanent layout and can be downright dangerous on model railway layouts because of the close proximity of electricity.

Preparation of the watercourse bed also involves colouring. If you think logically about real water, it is in its natural state a colourless liquid for the most part, yet every river, pond or lake takes on a vast range of colour arising from a variety of influences - I referred earlier to drainage water down cliffs and rock faces being discoloured with, for example, iron oxide, giving the distinct red/brown colour. Such dissolved minerals from the ground over and through which the water passes from its source will colour the water, but despite this the water itself remains translucent, so you can't just paint its top surface! From my own observation, that sort of colouring would usually found in very slow-flowing streams, ponds, bogs or seepages rather than in large areas of water. The Bridgewater Canal at Manchester, however, is a famous exception, where the water is very definitely 'rusty'.

Plant life, mud and debris also affect the colour, as does the colour of the rock over which the river may be flowing. Objects and general debris, particularly in urban areas, also affect the colour by reflecting, for example, overhanging trees, vegetation and structures. The surface of still water can act almost like a mirror of its surroundings, while disturbed surfaces alter the reflection, as near an obstruction in an otherwise slow-moving river where the flow of water is faster; water being forced against rocks, down waterfalls and the like creates a creamy whiteness.

The next step therefore is to decide what kind of water you want to represent on the model, refer to the real thing and try to copy the visual effects you see. First the watercourse bed should be given a coat of appropriate paint and sand, crushed stone, boulders, old wheels, tyres, barrels or whatever, glued into place. Tall weeds and rushes can be made from twists and clumps of bristle or similar material and placed in position with a touch of glue - for a really superb detail effect try the Scale Link etched bulrushes and vegetation - expensive and time-consuming, but well worth the effort on a visually important part of the layout foreground. Build up the edges with stone or mud and reeds, etc - don't just have a plain line between the adjacent grass and the substance you are using to represent the water.

Mention of the substance used to represent the water brings me on to the choice available for this purpose. I have often used varnish, clear gloss - have you ever seen matt water? - poured carefully over the appropriate area to only a modest depth. Don't, whatever you do, try to pour out the depth you require in one go - when eventually it dries out it will shrink and crack. I find it is best to build up the required depth and colour with several layers, allowing each to dry thoroughly - usually for a couple of days!

You can vary the colour a little, highlighting areas such as adding white for foam around rocks or creating the impression of deepening water away from the 'shoreline' by feathering the colour into the water for a short depth. New rocks or debris can be added at each layer, as can vegetation; when a layer is almost dry you can rough it up little to represent rough water and add touches of white for the bubbles of effervescence. You can arrange old barrels and debris (leftovers from plastic vehicle kits are a good source) to have these semi-submerged.

Varnish, even clear varnish, used this way always has a certain brownish tint, which I find is perfect for stagnant ponds or slow streams. It is best not used for very deep water, but to represent shallow or quite small areas.

For large, deep areas or where very detailed water is required, clear casting resin sold by artists' shops for embedding coins or other objects is ideal. It is quite expensive and crystal clear by comparison to the varnish, but don't use it clear - when did you last see crystal clear water naturally? Colour it in the mixing with enamel or acrylic paints and paint the surface below and between each layer of resin - yes, even casting resin is, I find, best applied in layers. It provides an ideal substance in which to embed detail, plant vegetation and debris.

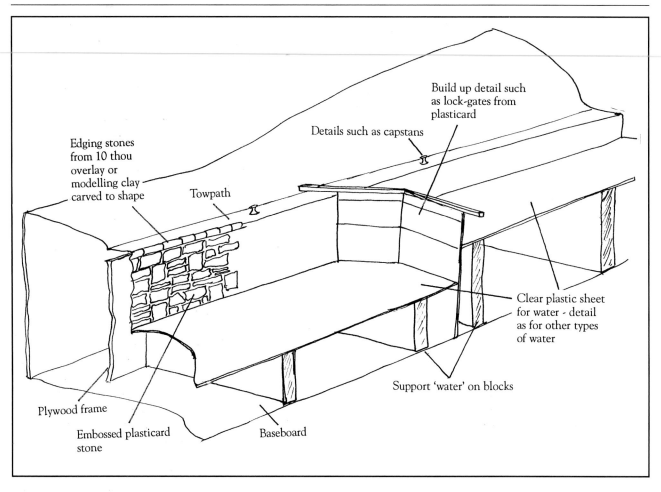

Build up detail such as lock-gates from plasticard

Details such as capstans

Edging stones from 10 thou overlay or modelling clay carved to shape

Towpath

Clear plastic sheet for water - detail as for other types of water

Support 'water' on blocks

Plywood frame

Embossed plasticard stone

Baseboard

Modelling water in canals and mill lodges, etc, requires a different approach from streams and rivers, since it is deep, of regular width and often surrounded by walling. Here are some details for modelling a canal lock, but the same principles would apply to a mill race, etc.

However, even for 'deep' water I would not try to mould it any deeper than say 1 inch, and it is seldom necessary to go beyond half this. To represent deep water you really need to create an *illusion* by colouring the base and the layers.

Because canals and mill lodges and races are man-made and usually incorporate some form of mechanical support such as sluices or lock gates, they require a different approach, and the sketch above shows how I set about modelling these. This approach using the clear sheet as a base is also suitable for other large types of water we have considered, but I believe really comes into its own for deep unnatural water and large lakes. The same suggestions, however, apply in respect of colouring the bed, and it is also possible to add to the effect by washing the underside of the clear sheet with a thin mix of the appropriate colour. You can also, of course, add either varnish or resin to the sheet, which makes it easier to embed detail. One big enemy of model railways is dust. The glossy finishes used to represent water seem to show it up, and the clear plastic sheets seem particularly bad in this respect.

I have not personally modelled a sea or beach scene. It has been done, but on only a couple of occasions can I recall it being done effectively. It would be necessary to build up waves gently leading to rocks or to a beach, and I would approach this using filler applied with a palette or table knife spread over the surface, smooth away from the land and creating a ripple or wave effect as it gets nearer the land. I would then paint it before applying a coat or two of casting resin. Where water comes up against a cliff or wall the colouring of the sea bed needs to be darker, or a narrow band, gradually lightening as you come away from it.

I have recently become acquainted with a substance known as acrylic gloss medium. It is a white gunge that dries crystal clear and is, I believe, used by artists to give protective coatings to their work. Being quite thick it can be spread with a palette knife to create ripples and irregularities, stippled and played around with for texture, and several coats can be built up - it appears too good a material to be true!

Earth, grass and crops

When we begin to look at how to represent grass and fields and various forms of vegetation a whole world of potential and experiment is opened up. If you add the making of trees and bushes, which we will deal with separately later, then you could almost devote an entire volume to bucolic scenery-making.

It is not very long ago that you could nip down to your local model shop, collect a few bags of dyed sawdust and a bag of lichen, and you had the basis for scenic modelling. The dyed sawdust was scattered on to glued or painted hills and fields and the lichen was stuck down in rows to represent hedges and individually for bushes and shrubs - it was glued to twigs to represent trees.

Thankfully those days have passed and a little more thought usually now goes into creating model landscapes. There is also now a wider range of scenic products and we have learned to borrow ideas from modellers in other fields, particularly the military modeller and diorama builder, and to take on board and develop the very advanced ideas that have developed elsewhere, particularly in the USA. As I said at the outset, it does strike me as being rather potty to spend considerable effort, time and money in acquiring or building superb models of locomotives and rolling-stock if you are going to use them in a landscape on which no trouble or thought has been expended.

The approach adopted in these volumes has been one of careful design, preparation and planning, and aiming for a 'holistic' approach and the general impression created rather than concentrating on one particular aspect of the model at the expense of others. As I have said, it is my view that creating a model railway is a bit like painting a three-dimensional picture with movement, and while detail is important it is the whole impression which is created that matters.

Having got the sermon out of the way once more, let's return to the grass roots - literally.

In the smaller scales it is usually sufficient to apply some form of scenic dressing scattered over a prepared surface - but not the dreaded dyed sawdust. There are now a variety of scenic dressings available made from other materials. I tend to use the vast Woodland Scenics range for most of my scenic materials. I know it is not the cheapest but it is the one that I have consistently found to give the best results from the point of view of both colour and texture. It is also quite adaptable to a variety of uses.

I think, particularly on large areas, that the colour of the surface beneath the grass and foliage plays an important part in creating the overall effect. Accordingly I think the first stage should be to represent the soil itself. One easy way of doing this in 3.5/4 mm scale and upwards is to cover the appropriate area with an earth turf mix dressing and to follow this later when dry with a coating of turf grass mix of the appropriate shade applied to a surface coated in 50/50 diluted PVA woodworking glue. Try to get a colour for the soil that is appropriate to the area you are modelling. On chalk downlands I would tend to leave the white plaster coating, painting it with a wash of very light grey/yellow just to take the edge off the white, and apply my grass to this. The fine turf mixes are excellent for most general uses, and if applied over an earth mix a good texture begins to develop.

Once the basic coating is down and thoroughly dry you can begin to add detail. Coarse turf mixes can be applied, together with products from other ranges to add a different texture. Build up areas of coarse grass in this way and use the foliage matting to represent bracken and other low bushy growth such as gorse of the type often seen on embankments on the railway side of the boundary fence. You can detail this further by adding tiny dots of colour to represent flowers, for example yellow for gorse. Coarser growth can be developed either by overlaying the foliage mat and building up layers - expensive - or using rubberised horsehair matting or similar material and painting it to represent the woody growth, adding turf for the foliage.

There are also other types of scenic dressing on the market, and one that deserves a mention is sold under a variety of trade names but is most often seen in the continental ranges of scenic materials. It is a nylon or similar fibre in short strands, and is applied from a soft plastic or rubber applicator on to a glued surface. The fibres are literally puffed out from the applicator and stand erect in the glue, giving the effect of separate blades of grass; however, they are all of a uniform height and, perhaps worst of all, they come in very gaudy shades, which are not very realistic.

In O gauge I believe it is necessary to do a little more than just apply a scenic material - although I do believe, as described earlier, that it still plays a vital role. One way of providing an alternative source of grass is to look at the application of other types of material. Traditionally surgical lint has been a source of inspiration to those who wish to experiment and go just a little way beyond the use of scatter material. Sheets of lint are dyed an appropriate shade and, when dry, glued in place on the landscape frame. The material can then either be roughed up and trimmed as appropriate or be torn off, leaving tufts stuck in place which, with a bit of judicious trimming, gives a fair representation of meadow or grazing land. Further details and effects can be added to this using longer material for weeds, and detail such as bushes using

The rough and varied appearance of the grass in the fields behind the train is worth noting, especially by contrast with the grass and herbage between the track and boundary fence. Note also the use of old railway sleepers for fencing, which was quite common; usually the sleepers were fixed upright, abutting each other, but here is a variation showing equally spaced sleepers with pointed tops. *D. Hampson*

Translated to the model, this HO scale layout shows how different textures of scenic materials can be used to give different effects, from unkempt coarse grass to the finer cultivated earth in the centre. *Andrew Booth*

Rough grass and pasture made from green felt 'roughed up' as described in the text and supplemented with various turf textures for coarser vegetation. *Andrew Booth*

some of the coarse turf materials mentioned earlier. The addition in places of the finest materials can be effective in representing closely cropped and grazed areas - particularly helpful if you are going to plonk some sheep down later.

In O and HO gauge I have successfully used green felt to represent meadowland. One of the interesting side effects of using this is the effect it gives of the turf above a rock outcrop. You can buy felt material from craft stalls and dressmaker's shops either in squares of approximately 1 ft or off a roll. I prefer to buy it off the roll rather than have to piece together individual squares and try to hide the joins; I see no point in adding to the work required. It seems to come in fairly standard colours; those that I regard as being particularly suitable for modelling are olive green, bright green and tan.

First cut a piece of felt to cover the area that you wish to work on. Use a straight edge to match the baseboard edge as appropriate, but avoid straight edges elsewhere - they seldom occur naturally. Cut holes to allow the material to pass over rocks, etc, in the same way that you cut wallpaper to go around light-switches. When you are satisfied with the cut, ie that your felt covers what you want it to cover, it can be glued in place. I have found it is not necessary to glue it all over but to apply spots of either woodworking glue or contact adhesive to the landscape only, not the felt, into which the felt can be pressed. Be careful when you get to the edges - at the baseboard edge I would glue it all along, wiping away any excess, but where the felt ends adjacent to other scenic work apply the glue a little way in from the edge so that when the felt is pushed into place the glue doesn't ooze out, spoiling, for example, your carefully modelled cliff face! When you press the material into place make sure that it follows the contours of the landscape, and particularly that it is pressed into any depressions.

Leave the glue to dry thoroughly, then you can begin to consider the colour. Dabs of colour can be added at random - say, darker greens - but be careful not to clog the material. Paint very much diluted is best, and it also soaks into the material which is a help for what comes next. Also apply similar daubs of a lighter colour, such as cream/yellow, for the effect you want. If this seems strange and more like army camouflage, don't worry - it gets better later. For broad shade effects, spraying or rubbing large areas with chalk pastels also works well.

The next stage is to attack the material with a suede brush, teasing up the surface, pulling up individual and clumps of fibres. Keeping working on it until you have the effect you desire, using the sharp edge of a craft knife to cut and separate some of the clumps. Save the debris that collects in the bristles, as this can be stuck down later to create other effects. You will find that this action has blended the daubs of colour to give a good overall grassy colour. You can also again use scissors, knife and razor to cut down some of the threads and strands if you have gone too far. Don't forget to look carefully at the edges of the material - they may need a bit more work with the suede brush to help blend them in and disguise any hard edges.

Other materials can then be glued to the felt to create different effects and vegetation - tall grasses, clumps of reeds, gorse, bushes and shrubs, for example.

Coarse, unkempt, dense weeds can be represented by using coarse material such as the old type of carpet felt underlay, the felt-type pipe lagging or the material sold for sound insulation in cars. Rough it up, paint it, and add scenic scatter to represent the foliage. Rubberised horsehair can also be used for this type of effect.

From 3.5 mm scale upwards you can really have some fun trying to represent greenery on a more individual basis, and again it is a matter of experimentation. I have found that dried grasses and vegetation collected while out walking and some of the ornamental ferns such as asparagus grass sold by florists can be an ideal source for this. With a little judicious pruning with the craft knife, colouring and perhaps the addition of scatter material to represent flowers or foliage, great effects can be produced.

Coarser grassland and crops such as wheat can be represented with other materials. Some of the fur fabrics sold for children's toy-making can be used to represent long grass or cornfields. The difficulty with this sort of material is colouring it, since much of it is in very gaudy colours which may be attractive to children but certainly don't look anything like the colour of anything growing naturally that I have seen. It can be dyed, but it doesn't always take the colouring too well. I try and pick a colour as near as possible to something natural and work from there. One alternative to dyeing the stuff is to spray it. I have used car touch-up paint lightly played over the material when in situ, but you need to spray lightly to avoid clogging the fibres and to minimise any damage to the material from chemical reaction. If you have an air-brush or a spray gun, so much the better, as you can mix your own enamel or acrylics.

When the material is glued in place you can also attack it with scissors or a sharp knife to reduce it to the height you require - try, however, to avoid a uniform height or the creation of unnaturally regular patterns. You can even shave the material to represent close-cropped grass. Scatter material can also be applied by just touching the top with PVA glue and applying the scatter to represent grass or corn fields - yellow, for example, could represent oil seed rape.

Ploughed fields are easiest to represent by combing filler mix with a home-made comb similar to the type they sell with the flooring adhesives. Colour the material first to prevent the white showing through, then coat with glue and the appropriate soil dressing.

So far as vegetable crops are concerned, for large areas I would look at the coarse turf and foliage mats, cut these and play around to try and represent rows of a particular vegetable. For large areas it is a matter of creating an image, a suggestion as to what is growing, rather than trying to model individual plants. On small areas - allotments or station gardens, for example - it is another matter, where I think a bit more time and effort can be devoted to trying to create more detail and a cameo or feature for the layout. As with most modelling, I think it is really a question of understanting rather than trying to do too much and being too clever.

Tree and bushes, hedges and fences

Trees and larger bushes and shrubs are not the easiest of things to model. My approach is to try and get the overall shape and colouring to resemble something like the tree I am trying to represent rather than to model every branch and leaf as accurately as possible. Different species of tree have characteristic shapes and colours, apart from the obvious shapes of fir trees being different from your average deciduous variety.

There are a number of model trees on the market, but few really look much like any trees I have ever seen! The few varieties that approach a realistic shape are generally quite expensive and, even for the HO/OO gauge models for which they are commonly made, they tend to be a bit on the small side. They do, however, as mentioned earlier, provide an ideal source for small trees and bushes in the larger scales.

Some of the less convincing general trees can be pressed into service for large or dense areas, saving the more individual trees for the foreground and edges of the scene.

I have made quite extensive use of trees produced by a Welsh company known as BTA. They produce a range of what I call general trees that form an ideal filling, as well as tree kits based on etchings that are twisted into shape from the flat, painted and to which a nylon net type of material is added to represent smaller branches. This is touched up with glue and dipped into a tub of mixed coarse scenic scatter, and there you have it - a tree.

Some of the continental manufacturers also produce highly detailed trees, but they tend to be a little expensive and on the smallish side - overall size, not just height - which is quite important when considering modelling trees. A 50-foot birch tree would be some 13 inches tall in O gauge, and 8 inches tall in 4 mm scale. If you compare these heights to the heights of most of the buildings and other structures on your layout, you will soon see that true-to-scale model trees are more than capable of dwarfing everything. You might, and quite rightly, say that this is quite correct. However, place scale height (and spread) trees and buildings together on a model and I would suggest that they will not look right. The height I mentioned for the birch tree is only a typical height. If you add a branch spread of 4-5 inches per tree, you can soon see that they do tend to take over. Moreover, the birch is a fairly modest example - an oak commonly ranges between 80 and 130 feet high with a spread quite easily of 30 to 40 feet - some $12^1/_2$ inches by $6^1/_2$ inches in 4 mm scale at the minimum dimensions quoted!

You are therefore faced with a choice - no trees, small trees, or picking smaller species. You can't very well avoid trees of the type that grow in the area you are modelling and have any pretence at the holistic approach to modelling that has been discussed and suggested. The answer, as with many modelling problems, lies with care and compromise. My view is that the best way forward is to *suggest* the shape and character of a particular type of tree, and to model it to the dimensions you feel look right. After all, it is you that has to look at the finished scene. With large objects such as trees and buildings I usually take the view that some form of selective compression is necessary for these objects to look right. We will have a look at how this becomes an integral part of building construction later. I also believe that this becomes more significant the larger the scale of the model. The tallest tree I've modelled in O gauge, a broad-leafed deciduous, stands a shade over 10 inches. By far the most important asset in railway modelling is a good eye - it's far more important that it *looks* right than that it has exact linear scale measurement!

One of the important things to bear in mind with most model railways is the restricted space they occupy and the comparatively cramped feel - particularly exacerbated if we try to copy slavishly everything to scale. Part of the visual success of any model railway - and the larger the scale, the more important this is - is the need to give an illusion of space and to avoid the cluttered appearance. Hence it is often necessary to hint and suggest rather than present in full glory, and be very careful with the visual juxtaposition and location of main structures including trees and buildings,

The three stages in the construction of more detailed trees from kits as described in the text. I have successfully used those intended for smaller scales as young trees or bushes in larger scales. Their construction is straightforward and they are certainly worth the effort. *Author's collection*

These are typical of many of the model trees sold and while not always suitable for use as individual or specimen trees, they can be usefully pressed into service as a background to more detailed foreground specimens. *Author's collection*

Here we a full-size tree designed for smaller scales used very effectively as a small tree in a larger scale. The model 'pill box' is unusual, not commonly modelled; I was surprised to find a whole volume devoted to their design and construction. *Author's collection*

which can so easily dominate rather than become part of the scene. I don't think any item or area of man-made work on a railway should physically dominate the scene unless we wish to deliberately emphasise a feature.

If you decide to make your own trees, I employ several variants on the common theme of twists of wire of one sort or another. I have two basic versions depending largely on the materials available. Multi-strand metal cable, the thicker the better, is ideal if you can get hold if it. A suitable length is cut and the individual wires in the cable are wound in groups, depending on the thickness you want, and bent to form the main branches and any splits in the main trunk, etc. The branches are in turn similarly divided and wound until you get down to branches of a single strand of the cable.

Twist, shape, trim and bend this trunk until you get an outline of the tree you want. A simple reference book such as *The Observer's Guide to Trees* is very useful here.

When you are happy with the shape, you can begin the messy bit, adding the texture to the frame. There are a number of materials that can be used for this, including interior filler and modelling clays - I even know of a modeller who uses the cheapest talcum powder he can find and mixes it with a loose paint, colouring the tree frame with the mixture! Whatever

you choose, you will I am sure evolve your own method and materials; several coats building up to the texture you require are better than trying one thick one. Paint can also be used to colour detail and bring life to the tree. Matt paint is essential, and greys rather than blacks as base colours. You can, incidentally, build up quite a detailed tree trunk using these methods - bark defects, bolls, and the effect of broken branches can all be developed in the 'mud' you apply to make the bark.

An alternative to multi-strand wire cable is the use of florist's wire; readily available from most florists, it is a thin soft wire that is easily bent. Bind lengths together to make up the trunk, bending out sections to make branches just as described for the multi-strand cable. Bind the wire together with tape from the bottom upwards and continue to wrap it up around the main boughs until they thin out.

Foliage couldn't be simpler. Foliage matting of the appropriate colour from the Woodland Scenics range is thinned out and teased into the shape you want, draped over the branches and held in place with touches of PVA woodworking glue. Ivy, moss and other growth can be added from other scenic materials such as turf mixes. In the larger scales, ivy and other climbing plants can be represented by the use of wire or thick cotton, painted, touched with glue, dipped into bowls of turf mix and twisted around the tree trunk, fence post or whatever. Touches of colour can be added to the foliage with paint to represent any flowers or blossom.

Modelling larger bushes and shrubs is also worth trying, particularly if they are treated carefully and a clump of lichen is not relied upon. For O gauge I have used some of the smaller detailed trees intended for 2 and 4 mm scales as bushes. Usually all that is required to convert them is the reduction in length of the main trunk to make it more bush-like, and the tweaking of some of the branches. Saplings and young trees can also be represented using these, but without the need for surgery. Some of the better and more expensive products intended for N gauge can be used for OO and HO models.

Plant your trees and bushes carefully - look at the real thing and see how the ground beneath trees, particularly large shady trees such as oaks and beeches, is often devoid of any proper grass, but soil and moss is often present, broken branches may litter the ground and roots can often be seen pushing through the top surface. Pay particular attention to the state of the trunk as it leaves the earth - it doesn't stand in a blob of glue looking like the base of a telegraph pole!

Similarly, look at how the grass and vegetation grows around the base of hedgerows and try to capture this using coarse turf materials and by suggesting individual

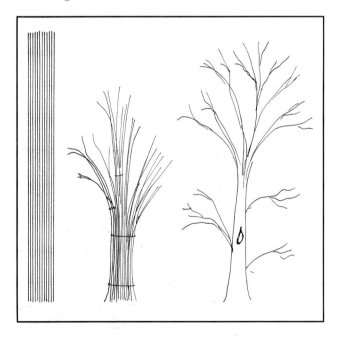

Making trees from wire. First take a bundle of, for example, florist's wire or multi-strand cable, and twist and bend it into a tree shape with trunk and branches, binding thicker pieces with wire hoops. When you are satisfied with the shape, coat the trunk and main boughs with your chosen material, detailing it with bolls, etc. Finally paint the tree and add foliage as described in the text.

There is a common misconception that the countryside is neat and tidy, a bit like its 'chocolate-box' image, but nothing could be further from the truth, as those who move from town to country often find. This view of an old implement store/barn is much more like it! The tin roof is interesting - modelling these is referred to later when we consider buildings (pages 61-62). *Author*

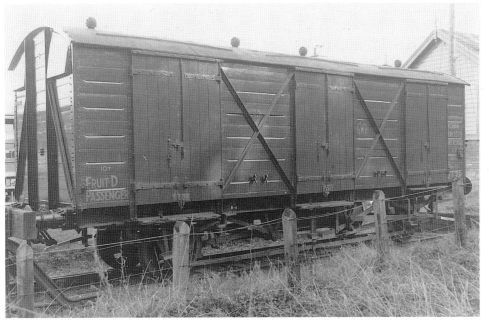

Even modern machinery misses cutting grass around the edges of fields, and usually beneath fences there is coarse grass such as that shown here. Coarse turf materials, dried grasses and rubberised horsehair can all be used to represent this. *Author's collection*

A similar fence and representation of coarse grass beneath it is seen here in the foreground in model form. Note also how standard model trees can be used as a background, with more detailed specimens in the foreground, the whole merging well with the real thing in this outdoor photograph. *Author*

tall grass clumps and other plants. Grass under fences even in mowed fields is usually longer, left uncut even in the days before machinery was used for cutting!

Hedges make a considerable visual impact and come in a variety of plant species made up of various shapes. While you can buy ready-made hedges, they are rarely convincing and I consequently prefer to make my own - a simple task. The basic material to use is rubberised horsehair cut roughly into strips of an appropriate height and width. Avoid straight cuts and straight tops unless you are representing a modern hedgerow that has recently received the attention of a tractor-driven cutter or a carefully manicured example of topiary at a cottage or park.

The horsehair material is painted a dark grey to represent branches and woody growth - spraying is easiest. Cut sufficient lengths for the area you are working on. Paint some PVA glue on the top and two thirds of the way down each side and dip each strip into a bowl of coarse scenic scatter of the appropriate greens.

Note that I say 'greens', plural - foliage is *not* of a uniform hue. Leave this to dry, then shake any excess back into the bowl and glue the hedge strip down. If you lose some foliage in planting the hedge, don't worry - it can be patched up when in situ. Similarly, if the hedge requires further trimming or needs to be made a bit more irregular, tear or cut a bit out and apply some more foliage to the bare bit after coating the area with glue.

Brief reference only is required on the subject of fencing. Unless you want to model a particular type, most requirements are catered for in proprietary products for the popular modelling scales ranging from post-and-rail boundary fences to cast concrete station fencing.

One crucial point with fencing is the need to try and ensure, unless you want to create a special effect, that the posts are upright; however, the rails should not be horizontal but follow upwards or downwards the contours of the ground.

One type of fence that I haven't yet managed to model satisfactorily is barbed wire. Etchings are available but I have never managed to get it looking right. I have used grey cotton, which is OK in the smaller scales but doesn't quite have enough detail for me, and I don't fancy trying to represent the barbs with touches of glue!

Fences and hedgerows are particularly important because they are very convenient for breaking, visually, a layout into sections or adding a dimension to a large open space. They are also a good way of disguising joints between baseboards and scenic mats, etc.

Brick walls are dealt with later when we look at

Iron railings and a tall solid wooden fence in a fascinating urban railway setting. Note the form and texture of the mini-cutting beneath the railings. The advertising hoardings are interesting and well worth modelling. *D. Hampson*

An alternative to iron railings or concrete slabs for platform fencing, post-and-rail fencing is easily constructed from balsa, with plasticard for the lower rails. The building, incidentally, is a model of a Colonel Stephens tin shack. *Author*

buildings and other structures. However, dry-stone walls may be appropriately dealt with here. There are various detailed mouldings available, some plastic, some plaster, which are fine for short sections on level ground. Otherwise I don't think there is really an alternative to making your own. One quick and simple method is to roll out lengths of modelling clay and mould this by hand to an appropriate shape, then add it to your layout and carve the stonework into it, painting when dry. The best method of all is to lay your own, stone by stone - ideal for larger scales, but an exercise that is tedious, time-consuming and one that can be overdone!

All of these suggestions for developing scenic effects are just that - suggestions. Scenic modelling is a very individual activity, and what one modeller swears by another will swear at. What it does offer is a wonderful opportunity to experiment and develop your own ideas, perhaps building on or adapting some of these suggestions rather than slavishly copying what someone else has done. It is surprising how often some of the best effects are discovered by accident.

Dry-stone walls vary in type depending on their location. Compare this Cotswold example with those from other parts of the country illustrated elsewhere in this book. *Author*

3.
THE URBAN SCENE

This chapter relates to the development of more urban scenery and the construction of buildings and other structures, in many instances those on the project layout, Platt Lane, which is the guinea pig for these methods.

The Platt Lane layout was conceived specifically to demonstrate modelling techniques and approaches, and it had to meet a number of criteria that I guess would also be considerations to many modellers. The layout had to be portable for exhibition use, capable of being fitted into the average domestic environment, and as realistic as possible commensurate with packing as much railway and scenic potential as possible into the space available - a tall order!

The philosophy behind the layout really demanded that a suitable prototype was searched out for modelling and adapted to suit the physical restraints imposed. The premise I adopted was that it would be impossible, indeed, if truth were told, not desirable, to model a prototype location even if space were available. To make the model as effective as possible, however, we needed to model the real thing, not other models or based on some Utopian belief in what a railway was like. So, if we are not able to model a prototype exactly, but wanted to model the *real* railway, what do we do? Simple - compromise, find potential scenes from reality, mix and match *appropriate* details to develop a believable model, and create a visual impression of the railway scene we wanted. Regardless of period, region, stock, even county, the approach is just as valid.

The task, therefore, was to search out, locally or in the area we wanted to model, suitable prototypes from which inspiration could be drawn. I highlighted a number I had found in my locality in the previous book, *Baseboard Basics and Making Tracks*, and that volume also explained in great detail how to draw from reality to develop a plan for a model railway and how that plan should include developing a design for

the project in totality from baseboards to operation.

In this volume we are looking at the development of the scenic or visual side of things, but the same principles of looking at reality for inspiration apply, whether it is a tree or a building. The trick is to assemble them as nature, the railway engineers or other builders would have done - that is, in a manner that is feasible and above all believable. It is about the avoidance of putting buildings and landscape together in a manner that just would not happen. It is about creating that elusive impression and feeling when you look at the model railway layout that everything is OK, that nothing looks out of place - nothing stands out as being glaringly wrong or irregular. This whole approach will later be carried through into the operation of the layout and the formation of the trains and choice of vehicles that run on it.

Platt Lane: adapting reality to the model

As we know, for Platt Lane I took for my inspiration Great Moor Street station in Bolton, an LNWR terminus, the second major station in the town but one that never really prospered, at least so far as passenger services were concerned. An LNWR incursion into the heart of L&Y territory, the latter's Horwich Works, Aspinall's empire on the L&Y, was but four miles or so away. I have included an early, rather poor-quality but nonetheless interesting overall view of the station in its surroundings to give the feel, the atmosphere, of what we are trying to re-create.

The multiple levels, with the railway on an embankment, demanded provision in the baseboard design for the many scenic features that were incorporated, and this provided the foundation, literally, of much of the scenic development we will be looking at.

The station building at Great Moor Street, the

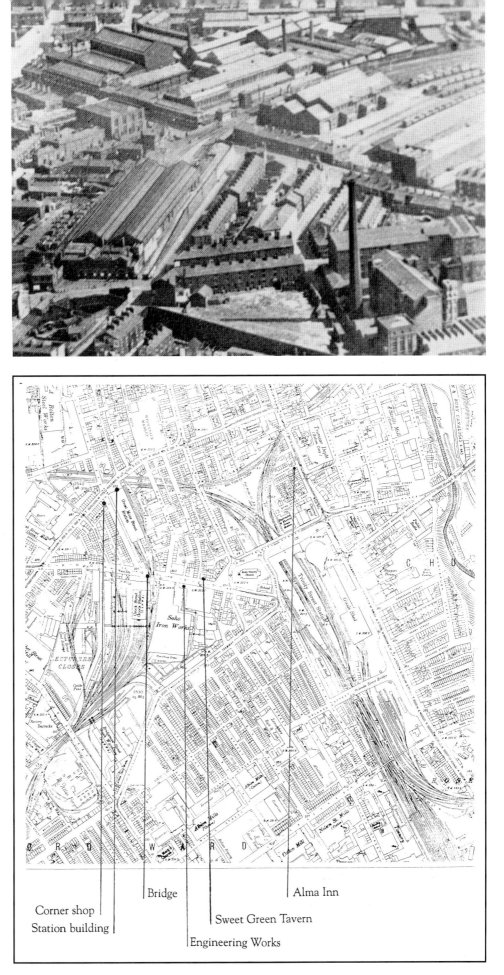

An early bird's eye view of Great Moor Street and the surrounding area. Despite its comparatively poor quality I thought it worthy of inclusion. *Author's collection*

Map of Bolton showing the locations of the original buildings on which the layout buildings were based, and their original positions in relation to Great Moor Street.

Bridge

Alma Inn

Corner shop
Station building

Sweet Green Tavern

Engineering Works

concept of the railway above street level and a surrounding of industrial premises and terraced housing provided the opportunities to develop little cameos, perhaps in surrounding areas away from the railway, thus lessening its impact on the total scene. Detailed allotments are just one idea that spring to mind.

One interesting feature of the real station was the siting of coal drops parallel to the platforms, an unusual feature at a north-western town station. I based my design around this, but having since found further information and studied the layout, I remain a little unsure as to whether the coal drops really work or not.

The layout was first exhibited at the Bolton Model Railway Exhibition and it was amazing how many people instantly thought they recognised a model of Great Moor Street station, despite the modifications undertaken. Literally dozens referred to memories and recollections of the station and its surroundings, and some swore to having worked in adjacent factories and offices. There is a moral here and I leave you to draw your own conclusions. Suffice to say that while the buildings are all models from the surrounding area, the only one that is in anything like its real location, albeit reduced in size, having lost a few windows and offices, is the station building itself!

How the layout developed in terms of the design of the scenic side needs to be considered before we look at the construction of individual buildings, as this philosophy is fundamental to the whole approach to the layout, and mine to building model railways. Whatever prototype, location or nationality is the source of your model railway, it will be so much the better for being based on reality, even if it is not a model of a particular station.

Reference to the real thing is a recurring theme and one that I feel cannot be over-emphasised, whether it is in relation to the development of a track plan or the road vehicles, even the people themselves and their clothes. All the ingredients of a model railway need to be contemporary, appropriate and consistent with reality to achieve the impression we are trying to create.

You can quite easily develop a basic plan for your model railway using the real thing as a model - we looked at this in detail in the previous book. How, for example, some railway companies favoured certain types of layout and how, if you have regard to these, you can start to create the right impression and feel. This theme continues all the way through the building of the model railway.

There are features typical of one or another company in the way in which basic facilities are constructed, such as platforms, styles of architecture on a particular route such as the Settle & Carlisle or the Bedford to Bletchley line. You, indeed the majority of the viewers

of your layout, might not know of these subtleties, but they are important to the total picture that is created by the model. Similarly, you might not appreciate the subtleties of architecture or landscape in your own area, which you might see every day, but you would soon know if there was a change or something wasn't right - the same is true of the model. All this development of the picture we are creating occurs before the obvious giveaways such as signals or trains are in place on the layout. One of my favourite views expressed on model railway building is along the lines of: 'You should on viewing a model railway be able to tell without signals and rolling-stock where it is supposed to be located, and the period at which it is set. Not the exact year or town, but the area - South Devon, West Yorkshire, etc.'

With the Platt Lane layout I had already planned that to maximise the space on the layout for operation, the station building would be built on its own discrete unit which could be bolted on to the layout for exhibition use, and act as a little diorama in itself at other times. Because a station building to suit the layout was also going to be rather large, especially in O gauge, I felt also that it was wise to have the building as a separate unit for ease of transportation - remember that the layout was intended to be portable for exhibition use.

The source of inspiration, then, was Bolton Great Moor Street and its environs, but as you would need considerable space - about the size of an average village hall - to model it, it would not be possible for the finished model to be more than a passing resemblance. However, by taking ideas and features and adapting them to the space available and designing the layout around this choice, it should be possible to end up with a layout that is believable and does not contain too many irregularities to spoil the impression.

Clearly, the main station building from Great Moor Street was an unusual structure. Having spoken earlier about the need to be consistent in the choice of material for a layout, as railway companies developed their own 'house styles', this station building was, so far as I can ascertain, a one-off - a one-off on the fairly standardised LNWR, and a one-off amongst standard LNWR material elsewhere around the railway.

Immediately, you hit a fundamental problem when modelling large structures and particularly buildings - their sheer size and bulk. This problem seems to get worse the larger the scale. I have generally found even in N gauge, particularly with large structures, that if they are modelled to their scale size they do not look right. I suspect that this has much to do with the way in which we normally see large structures as opposed to the angles at which models are commonly viewed, coupled with the amount of a scene that the human

Four stages in the development of the Platt Lane station building. The first (*right*) is a 1962 view of the original, Great Moor Street. *D. Hampson*

Below This is where we start to turn the 'research' into the model. I have discussed at length my approach with regard to things *looking* right and the help provided by mock-ups of buildings, etc, in finalising arrangements without risk of wasting work on finishing models that don't eventually look right on the layout. This was the first mock-up of the station building (platform-side view) with various notes and measurements scribbled on. *Author*

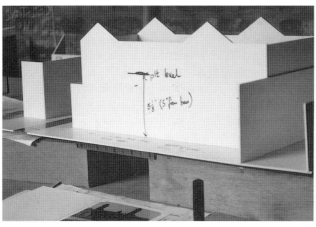

Above The frontage of the station building during construction, and still bearing the name of its inspiration. Note how the building has been adapted from the original, with certain parts omitted and reduced over all in size. The method of construction used was as described in the text - plasticard on a shell of featherboard, which had formed the mock-up. Note that the detail is built up from plasticard with castings for the awning brackets and, yet to be added, the chimney pots. *P. Smith/Kirtley Models*

Left The completed station building module, complete with its own pavement and the adjoining shops. *Author*

The process of checking the 'look' of the overall layout by the use of mock-ups of buildings and other features has begun even as the track is still being laid. I find it therapeutic to be able to move from one aspect of modelling to another, which is helped if you have thought out your intentions before you begin - a key demand advocated in this series of books. The very rough building mock-ups seen here are, from left to right, the 1950s office block and engineering works, and, just visible at the extreme right of the picture, the Sweet Green Tavern. *Author*

eye takes in. Whatever the reason, however, we still need to build the models and get them to look right. You will see from the illustrations that although I knew broadly what buildings were going to be placed where on the model, which was part of the planning and design process, I began by experimenting with simple mock-ups of the types of buildings.

Often what looks fine on a plan or mock-up needs to be amended when the final model is developed. Because so much time is invested in building models, a little extra time spent in planning and preparation, building mock-ups, and checking and re-checking the impression given, is worth a little bit of extra effort if it results in a better overall model. Consequently, before the baseboards were built a cardboard mock-up of their intended construction was built to a quarter scale. Similarly, mock-ups of the buildings were made.

The station building had to be reduced in size, not just because of this problem with scale, but because it spanned fewer tracks than in the prototype. Selective compression was therefore the next stage. The photographs on page 41 show how, for example, the building was reduced along its frontage by leaving out certain sections. This did not, however, solve the problem entirely, because visually the building was still too large. It therefore needed to be reduced a little in height, width and depth, with commensurate reductions in the dimensions of the windows, doors, etc - effectively an overall scaling down of the whole.

This is not a problem just with larger buildings, but also arises with smaller ones. The small Kent & East Sussex tin-shed station building shown in some of the illustrations was reduced similarly all round to enable it to look right on the layout. The benefit of the

mock-up is felt here - a simple 'cornflake packet' structure can be cut to the scale size of the building being modelled and placed on the layout, studied for a while, removed, reduced all round by a small amount, then replaced - a process repeated until the right proportions had been reached. This is not something that you could - indeed, would want to - do with a finished model.

The area at the front of the Platt Lane layout around the coal drops pretty well takes care of itself. The area behind the railway, beyond the platforms, I had originally intended would be a row of terraced properties, the upper floor windows being level with the top of the rear wall of the station. I wasn't sure at first whether to model the frontage of the terrace, with some shops and all the potential for detailing that went with them, or to model house backs with all the potential for detailed back yards. Either would have resulted in a lot of effort and work that would not have been too obvious because of the location. Incidentally, terraced houses occupied the equivalent site at the original Great Moor Street. Imagine a solid brick wall 40 feet from your bedroom window! Even if it was an LNWR-built wall supporting some of Britain's finest railway locomotives and stock, it would hardly be the sort of thing to appear in an estate agent's blurb.

I was intending to model some industrial/factory-type buildings on the opposite side of the roadway that passes beneath the railway at the rear of the layout, and had begun looking around the area for suitable inspiration. There is locally a large engineering firm with its origins going back to the 18th century, which also had strong connections with the early railway

Right I make no apologies for showing in this and the next few pictures what might be called source material. Although these are mostly older views, it is surprising what can still be found in 'original' condition despite 20 and more years of demolition and modernisation. The pictures show the variety of style and materials of once commonplace functional architecture, terraced housing and shops, essential on any model railway representing all but the most rural of scenes. This picture shows typical housing of the area on the Great Moor Street approaches about half a mile or so from the station. The stone setts, pavement, footbridge and the costume of the ladies should be noted. *Bolton Local History Library*

Right Photographs such as these are invaluable for modelling shops of the 1920s. The signs and display are typical of newsagents, if rather untidy. The newspaper hoardings could date the picture accurately, although I haven't tried! The pavement stones are unusual, apparently laid in 'columns'. *Author's collection*

Left Moving on a few years, here are typical shops in the 1950s. *Author's collection*

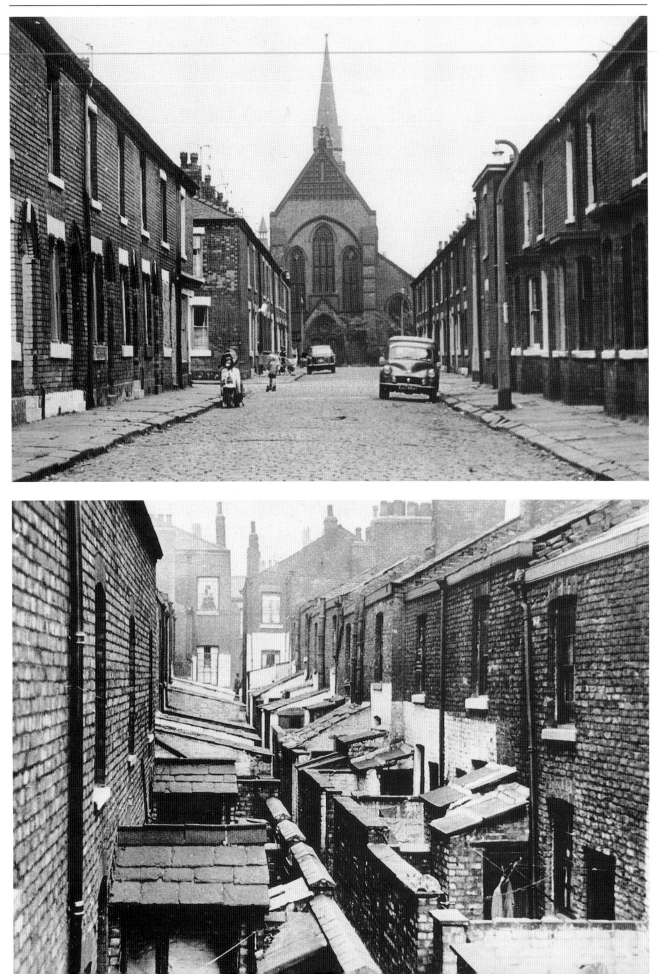

Opposite page As railway modellers we often tend to shrug off reality, and prefer shiny engines, and pristine houses and gardens. Railway journeys in urban areas, even today, take the traveller through tracts of what can only be described as the less desirable areas of towns and cities. These 1960s photographs show front and rear views of terraced houses - a mine of detail from crumbling brickwork to washing and the Morris Minor van. Note the different styles within the same street and the church at the end. God or the workplace was seldom far from view in these areas. *Author's collection*

Derby Terrace

Above and left Similar terraced houses have been included on the Platt Lane layout, and are seen here under construction and complete. Detail such as dustbins, the gable-end advert, the chalked wickets and 1950s graffiti all help to create the impression and period of the model - but shouldn't be overdone! *P. Smith/Kirtley Models; Author*

history, being a manufacturer, *inter alia*, of steam locomotives. A 1950s brick and glass office block is married to one of the older parts of the building, and thoughts turned to using this as the basis for filling that site and hinting, probably in half relief, at the main engineering shops behind. However, further examination of the adjacent, original, building revealed not only an attractive brick frontage with a classic works entrance gate in the middle, but also an interesting roofline that could be simplified and modelled. Adapting this to fit the site behind the platform would provide not only an interesting building, but

because of the roofline and detail would also add interest at the right level commensurate with the station walls in front of the site on the layout; as I mentioned earlier, these would obscure the view of the lower two-thirds of any model located there.

I have included some pictures showing this building and the model under construction. I also included earlier a map showing the location of Great Moor Street and the buildings that were used for inspiration for the Platt Lane model to show how suitable structures were repositioned to suit the layout. I would recommend this approach providing that you choose

Left The full frontage of the engineering works used as the basis for the model. Excluding the modern office block just visible at the extreme left, to model this in O gauge would require something in the order of 6 feet. And that would be without the Sweet Green Tavern, which in reality is across the road, but in the model I felt was more appropriate at the opposite end of the facade of the office block. For the model the frontage was subsequently condensed to around 4 feet. *Author*

Hargreaves Works

Below Roof detail and original features from the engineering works. Gutters, boarding, slate roof, roof-lights and cat-walks are just some of the details revealed that could prove useful in modelling this type of building. *Author*

Above Part of the mock-up of the model of the works, comprising the main gate and adjoining offices. Note that it was made in sections for ease of manoeuvring; they were subsequently joined together to become the base for the model, one advantage of using featherboard for the mock-up.

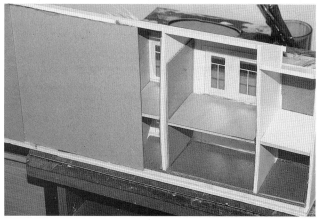

Above The model takes shape. Note the corrugated card bracing in the form of walls and floors. Odd bits of card were used to blank off the back - the appearance at the rear is not too important.

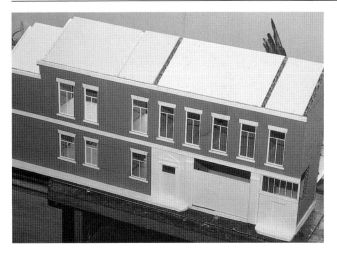

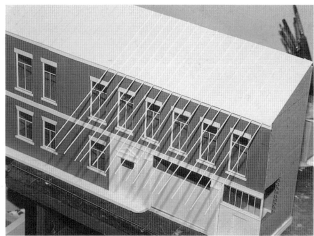

In this view the front walls are being built up, and the roof base is in position.

The 40 thou plasticard roof is now in place, and microstrip is being added to represent the roof battens, trimmed to length later.

This section is complete, the roof finished and ready for painting.

The completed sections placed together with the pub prior to painting.

I have an aversion to cleanliness on models, hence the weathering applied to the factory. The lettering is plastic and is glued on. The camera flash reveals the interior of the rooms, whereas to the naked eye the windows appear black.

Details of the factory roof - compare with the photo of the real thing opposite.

All model photos P. Smith/Kirtley Models

your buildings carefully and put them in a position on the layout that is credible rather than just where you fancy or where they fit. Remember, it is the overall impression that counts. At the risk of being repetitive, the key point in choosing your buildings is that they should fit the location and period being modelled. Just as you wouldn't run a train of British Rail Mark III coaches hauled by a 'Dean Goods', so you wouldn't want a row of Yorkshire weavers' cottages on a layout set in Sussex! It is not difficult to find suitable buildings to model, and in the examples I have used I have plundered the same area from which the idea for the railway itself was based.

There are numerous books on vernacular, industrial and local architecture of various parts of the UK (and overseas!), and albums of Victorian and Edwardian photographs to draw from for your information if you cannot visit a particular area. When it comes to railway architecture there is an ever-increasing range of books on railways with good-quality photographs and often drawings of railway architecture. I can readily call to mind books on LMS, GWR, SE&CR and SR concrete architecture and products. Additionally many of the line histories produced in recent years contain drawings as well as excellent photographs.

I would not be tempted to design my own buildings, but rather to adapt a prototype to suit a location on the model. Not surprisingly, perhaps, models developed from 'own designs' tend to look unconvincing - anyway, you wouldn't design your own locos and stock, would you?

Further buildings on the Platt Lane layout come from the general area of the town, and I have included photographs of both model and prototype. The Sweet Green Tavern, for example, is across the road from the engineering works and now stands in splendid isolation with adjacent terraced housing having been demolished to make way for some grass and concrete landscape that needs regular maintenance and cleaning - I believe it's called progress! However, I digress. The building has been modelled as it was in the late 1950s rather than in its rather more cleaned-up state of today. It was also moved to abut the engineering works.

The Alma Inn, on the other hand, is a totally different type of building and has similarly been relocated from nearer the town's L&Y station! I have also included photographs of the real thing and the model. There is no connection between the number of pubs on the layout and my drinking habits, merely a reflection of the pub-on-almost-every-corner situation that typified many inner city working class areas.

The shop adjacent to the station buildings was an integral part of the construction of the raised area on which the railway ran, and the side walls were a continuation of the retaining walls. These were built as

Two pubs are modelled on Platt Lane. This is the original for the Sweet Green Tavern. . . *Author*

part of the station building, but their use was changed. The shop at the other end of the station concourse was modelled from an old photograph of a row of shops and houses that had occupied a similar position at Great Moor Street until demolished in the 1950s. They were actually part of the continuation of Great Moor Street and were a bit unusual for the area. I was lucky enough to find pictures of both front and back, and because they show quite a lot of detail of life in the 1930s, when I believe they were taken, despite their less then perfect quality I have included them.

Other buildings, shops and terraces were taken from appropriate locations around and about the town - it is surprising how many buildings still exist in more or less their original state, perhaps with changed doors and windows above modern shop signs.

A common feature until a few years ago was advertisements painted directly on to gable end walls - if you look carefully you can still see faded reminders. One of these was an essential requirement for the Platt Lane layout, as was a good old-fashioned adver-

. . .and this is the model nearing completion, the roof panel having just been added. *P. Smith/Kirtley Models*

Sweet Green Tavern

The finished building in place. Although modelled faithfully, its position has been moved across the road to abut on to the engineering works. *Author*

tising hoarding placed near the coal yard entrance.

Other odd pieces of ground can be filled in with workshops, garages and allotments. There are some small allotments at the front of the layout across from the coal yard entrance, and for these I relied on the memory of hours spent with my father on his allotment which, luckily for me, adjoined the local goods yard. I spent many hours watching an Aspinall or '4F' shunting a few wagons - that site is now a school!

There is one 'foreigner' on the layout - across from the coal yard entrance is a cinema, typical of the small pre-Odeon 'flea-pits' that once abounded. There were

dozens of cinemas in Bolton at one time, and while many of them were photographed, the less significant, ordinary ones were not - a bit like photographs of railways where the ordinary humdrum essential items often missed the lens in favour of the glamorous and mighty. However, I did recall passing one in a town some 18 miles away which fitted my memories or this type of entertainment hall, still in more or less original overall state, and because it was of a rendered finish, there was little if anything to suggest a particular location in its architecture. It was duly photographed and became the basis of the model.

Left The Alma Inn is Platt Lane's other pub. Just look at the wealth of detail in the side alley just crying out to be modelled! *Author*

The Alma Inn

Below left The model frontage of the Alma Inn. Compared with the real thing, its appearance has been back-dated and the pub made somewhat worse for wear that it is today. *P. Smith/Kirtley Models*

Below The Alma Inn takes up its position on the layout. *Author*

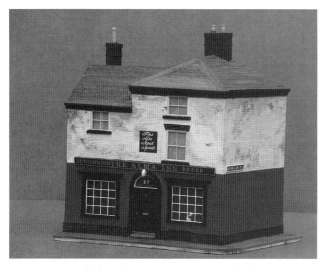

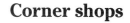

Corner shops

This row of terraced shops was adjacent to Great Moor Street concourse, which was off the picture in the left foreground. The shop fronts are typical and, subject to changing advertising, shop window displays, etc, could represent almost any period between the First World War and 1965. Note the unusual chimneys. I find a certain nostalgia in this, having spent much of my childhood living above such premises. The end shop has been modelled for Platt Lane. *Bolton Local History Library*

Right The rear of the same terraced shops prior to demolition; note the washing and the sleeper fencing. This view, taken around 1960, is at the start of the slum clearance era, and the openness of the rear is a result of such clearance. Worth noting is that modification has been made to the buildings; at least one window has been replaced from the original sash, and the small window halfway along suggests an indoor bathroom/toilet, although there is no soil pipe. This sort of detail and consistency is necessary to make models believable, rather than absolute adherence to scale dimension and the incorporation of every last 'nut and bolt'. *Bolton Local History Library*

Below The model end-of-terrace shop based on the corner shop from the row adjacent to Great Moor Street, pictured opposite.

The detail of the enamel signs, posters, boarded window opening and graffiti helps to add a touch of realism. *Author*

Below The completed shops adjacent to Platt Lane's concourse, showing some interior detail. Note the board with its effect of a torn-off poster - a nice touch of detail. *Author*

The basis of any shop display is a false back and bottom. In the larger scales ready-made castings are available for display material, augmented with signs, posters, etc.

Estate agents and similar require a simple plasticard structure, on which display cards are represented by scraps of paper cut and painted.

Plasticard is used to make supports and represent boxes for a fruit and veg display. Use scrap, fishing weights, etc, suitably painted, for the produce.

Newsagents displays are relatively easy - use paper or card to represent papers and magazines. Papers on racks outside the shop were common. Don't forget newspaper placards below the window.

Old hardware shops often had displays of tools in the window. Use detail castings glued to a plasticard back, and paint patches to represent seed displays, etc, or use posters or magazine cuttings. Fill the window bottom with offcuts of plasticard to represent packets, boxes, etc.

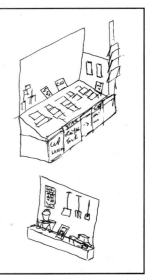

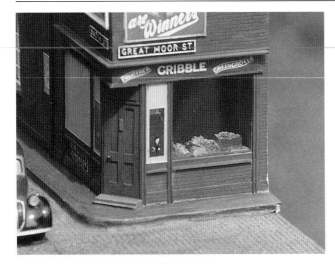

Above left and above Greengocer's and estate agent's windows on the layout built and detailed as described on the previous page. *Author*

Left Despite changes to shop fronts, additional advertising, etc, it is often possible to find out much about how buildings appeared when built or earlier in their lives by looking above the ground floor and sometimes down the side or at the back, where original features remain. *Author*

Below left and below Shop frontages were not the only location for advertising. Many local products were often advertised on gable-end walls and if we look carefully their remains can still sometimes be seen; they were quite complex, graphically speaking. The very faded example shown here was used as the basis for one on Platt Lane. There are a variety of ways of achieving this effect, such as experimenting with dry print transfers. *Author*

Regent cinema

The prototype Regent cinema and the completed model, resplendent in its grey rendering, as a contrast to all the brickwork on the layout. Note the corrugated roof weathered with readily available weathering powder. *Author; P. Smith/Kirtley Models*

Detail of the cinema entrance, real and model. The columns are adapted from cast gas lamps with the head removed and etched brackets added. The canopy is corrugated tin. *Author*

Constructing buildings

I discussed earlier the objective of giving the model railway layout its identity and location without the obvious railway features such as signals, locomotives and stock. Perhaps the single most important items in placing the layout in its geographical location and timescale are the buildings. It is therefore essential that they be treated with the same care, consideration and choice that we give to the locomotives and rolling-stock. This leads I suppose to considering how we turn our prototype sources into models for the layout. It's OK having a photograph, but how does it become a model?

Well, the first step is to identify the site for each particular model, establish the boundaries and give yourself a ground area plan from which to work. This helps in fitting the models in and determining their overall size. As I mentioned earlier, selective and pro-

portional reductions are often necessary to get a model building to look right, let alone fit a chosen site.

My next stage for almost any building is to draw a rough outline of the elevations, to scale, and to use this as the basis for a very simple cardboard mock-up. No roof or detail is necessary, but you can, if it helps, draw on windows and doors with a felt-tip pen. I find this invaluable not only for establishing how much a building may need to be reduced or modified to fit a site, but also to help get a feel as to how the layout will look, and whether particular features are going to work visually. I know it takes a bit of effort and time, but it is well worth it and saves the embarrassment of having something that either will not fit or does not look right after spending hours building and detailing it. I actually enjoy this aspect of planning, using mock-ups, moving them around, trying different locations and angles - you can dream and hope what it will look like even if the finished result doesn't quite

As we have seen, terraced houses come in a variety of shapes and styles. The one chosen for this site on the layout was a little unusual, with arrangements around the yard and extensions that indicate a better class and more modern building period, after the construction of the railway, perhaps to replace earlier properties. This view of the mock-up helps to show how these can be a vehicle for change; they indicate that originally a gable-ended rear extension was envisaged, and that the houses were stepped to cope with the slope. Locally this latter point was very rare and therefore not pursued. *Author*

match your aspirations. It's good to daydream sometimes - it helps keep the spirits up when things aren't going well!

When it comes to actually building the models it seems that there are almost as many methods and techniques as styles of architecture. As with other aspects of the hobby, every modeller seems to develop his or her own way of producing model buildings. I have already said that when it comes to modelling I am basically lazy and will take the easiest route to building things commensurate with achieving the overall effect I am aiming for. Accordingly I will concentrate on the methods that I use myself, and which were used on the project layout. The techniques and, more particularly, the materials do vary from scale to scale, and although the processes and techniques I describe are as common as possible, I will note where I reckon something is not suitable for some scales.

The point to stress once more before we begin is that it is the *overall impression and feel* being aimed for rather than a model that has every last nail and bolt represented down to the last speck of rust.

The Platt Lane buildings illustrated are in the main the work of Pete Smith of Kirtley Models, who specialises in producing models of buildings to commission. Pete's methods and approach are very similar to mine for O gauge, and through various articles, demonstrations and exhibitions Pete has made his methods and skills known to many. The photographs show broadly how the buildings were developed and I will describe the methodology and techniques behind their construction.

I think a note about tools is called for first. Basic hand tools are all that is required for making build-

ings, whatever materials you use. You will need a steel straight-edge end ruler; a sharp craft knife (a scalpel for preference, but do be careful as these are very *very* sharp); an endless supply of spare blades (they soon blunt after only a few cuts, and are then useful only as scrapers or for other non-cutting purposes - using knives with dull blades is a good way of cutting yourself!); a hard lead pencil (H or 2H) for marking out; a felt-tip pen, which is also useful; glues appropriate to the materials you are using; a small drill, preferably a 12-volt mini drill, and a selection of bits, burrs and cutting discs together with a cutting board or mat on which to work; and the usual selection of files, abrasive papers, paints, etc, that modelling requires.

The basic material used for the Platt Lane buildings is known under various trade names, but most commonly as 'featherboard'. It is widely used in advertising displays and shop-window dressing, and if you know anyone connected with that work, cultivate them because they may be a useful source of the stuff for perhaps no more than the price of the odd drink. If you need to buy it, a number of retailers now offer it in the modelling press. It is about one-eighth of an inch thick and is a foam plastic material sandwiched between an outer layer of fine white card. The material is lightweight, stable and strong, very easy to work, and does not appear to be affected by modelling glues, paint or humidity. It forms the basic shell of all but the smallest buildings on the layout, and can also be used for large buildings in the smaller 3.5/4 mm scales.

Detail layers representing brick and stone, etc, are added later, but before moving on to the outer skin we will look at a few alternatives for shells. In the larger scales, O and above, thin plywood of good quality can also be used, and is indeed a fairly traditional approach. Quite thin ply, down to a couple of millimetres, can be bought, intended for model boats; I have also used standard one-eighth-inch successfully. It is heavier than featherboard and not as easy to work, but certainly provides a strong, firm shell for larger buildings.

'Plasticard' can also be used most satisfactorily - 60 thou for O gauge and larger 4 mm structures to which detail is later added. For 2 to 4 mm scale, shells of a thinner material can be used and, indeed, some of the thicker embossed or moulded detail sheets such as the Wills Scenic Range can be used for small structures without a shell. Plasticard shells, like featherboard and ply, require interior walls, floors and partitions to maintain their strength and shape.

When you have worked out the dimensions of your buildings and the locations of windows, doors, etc, an outline plan should be prepared. Don't worry too much about dimensional accuracy - concentrate on getting the proportions right. You can also save a bit of time at this stage by drawing this on to the material you are using for the building's shell.

If you haven't got a scale drawing or can't visit and measure the buildings, don't worry - there are ways to overcome this problem. Where the subject of the model is a railway building you may be able to find a similar building in one of the railway histories referred to earlier. You can work out dimensions perhaps from standard buildings produced in appropriate style by your particular railway company - for example the LNWR wooden station buildings.

For other structures you can work out approximate dimensions - side-on photos of elevations are particularly helpful for this. Measurements can be estimated by reference to standard average dimensions. For example, bricks are commonly around 8½ in x 4 in x 3½ in (plus the mortar course), doors usually 6 ft 6 in tall. While you won't get exact dimensions to the last inch using this method, you should be able to get the proportions right. Try it on the 'cornflake packet' mock-up before you begin to make the actual model.

It is surprising what you can deduce from reference to photos. Don't rush in - check things out carefully and don't be too surprised if you find something unexpected in relation to the original purpose of the buildings. Adjacent land and property can also give valuable clues. Sometimes, for example, there are buildings adjacent to a pub that seem to have no connection with it and perhaps may now be small workshops or garages; these may have been stable blocks used by coaches, carters and travellers in the days before the motor car. Knowing this can help you deduce the plan of a model of that building.

You will need to draw these final deductions into the plans on the walls of your building's shell. When you come to the overall dimensions for walls, don't forget to allow for the width of your chosen shell material on the end walls. You will also need to mark out the door and window apertures, but don't forget to make them slightly bigger to allow for the frames if you use the building methods I am outlining. In O gauge 5 mm all round is about right.

Next cut out the walls and the openings, make up the shell and try it in place on the layout just to check it out again - I am almost paranoid about the impression something creates. Also don't forget that the overall size of the shell should be slightly reduced to accommodate any cladding that you will be applying.

While the shell is on the layout, on trial as it were, make absolutely sure that it looks right - stand back, leave it overnight, take another look, paying particular attention to whether it looks too dominant or insignificant. It is useful at this stage, if you can, to play around with several shells and perhaps other key features that may be around such as trees, bridges, cars, people and, particularly, trains. This stage is important because you can alter things now without too much angst - perhaps raise the height or shorten a wall. For example, with the Platt Lane engineering works the original had evidence of an extra floor, but we thought that on the model it would not look right. The mock-up, however, revealed that the answer wasn't quite so simple. We compromised - only one storey, but higher walls achieved by proportional increase in the height of brickwork between windows, and between windows and eaves.

The mention of eaves reminds me that many architectural terms are used to describe the detail products sold to develop our models. While some of those used are not always accurate, I have enclosed a few sketches overleaf showing some of the more common terms that are useful to us modellers.

Hot glue guns can now be purchased quite cheaply and are useful for featherboard and plywood. For plasticard I use good old Mek Pak, but you will no doubt have your own preference for polystyrene solvent. Not all the various types on the market will stick all plastic modelling materials. For example, Mek Pak will not fix some of the plastic mouldings such as Plas Struct used for details. This is because of the wide variety of types of plastic used for modelling products, so check that you have got the right solvent for the materials you are using. Be careful with these substances. If spilt, not only can they make a mess of models, but also carpets and furniture. They can also, if swallowed or inhaled, be dangerous to health, so *always read the labels carefully* regarding their use. Make sure your shell is correct and thoroughly fixed together before proceeding.

I always find that whatever the material that is

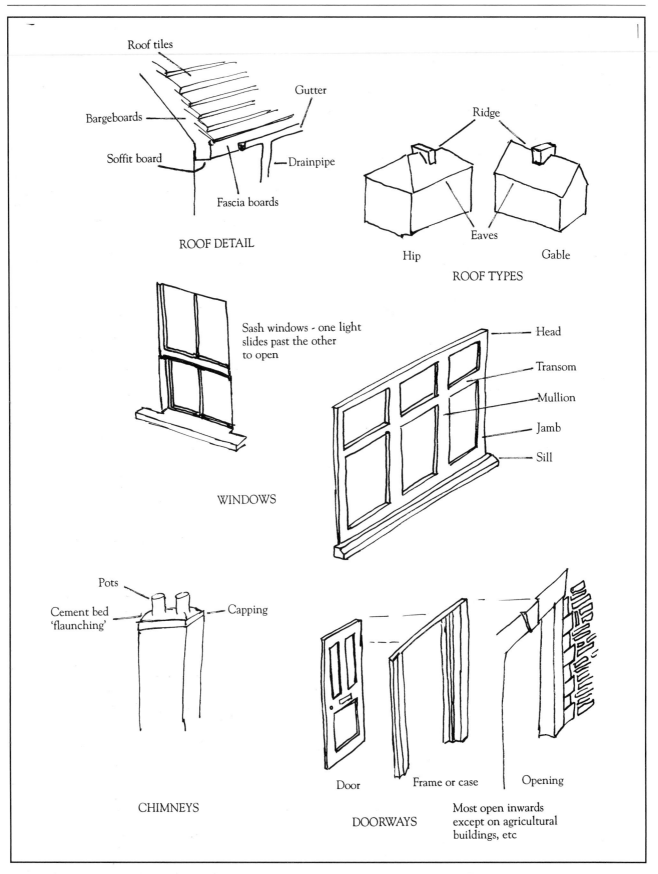

ROOF DETAIL

ROOF TYPES

Hip   Gable

Roof tiles

Bargeboards

Soffit board

Gutter

Drainpipe

Fascia boards

Ridge

Eaves

Sash windows - one light slides past the other to open

WINDOWS

Head

Transom

Mullion

Jamb

Sill

Pots

Cement bed 'flaunching'

Capping

CHIMNEYS

DOORWAYS

Door

Frame or case

Opening

Most open inwards except on agricultural buildings, etc

Architectural terminology

The basic shell of the terraced houses being detailed with plasticard and the beginnings of the roof detail - the paper has been ruled for the slates. Corrugated cardboard provided a good substitute for featherboard in the projecting rooms. The basic construction details can be seen. *P. Smith/Kirtley Models*

being used, it is as well for strength to build the shell around a floor. You can then add interior partitions and internal walls for additional bracing; further floors in multi-level buildings also help. I find it best to cut these out before the shell is assembled, as it is easier to measure the exact sizes required. Unless you are intent on modelling the interior, all you need to worry about with internal walls, etc, is avoiding doorways and window openings.

You next need to consider the cladding or finish, be it brick, stone, boarding or corrugated tin sheets. The scale in which you are modelling will to a certain extent dictate how you do this. For example, in O gauge an intermediate layer of 40 thou plasticard is used, to which the embossed sheet is added. It is necessary, however, that the openings are cut out to the correct finished size. In smaller scales you can get some good results with pre-printed and sometimes embossed stone cards and brick papers. I have to confess that I don't get on with these materials - I couldn't even manage the cardboard cut-out models on cornflake packets!

I don't often use the embossed material intended for the scale I am working in. It rather depends on the model and location, but, particularly in O gauge, I find some of the embossed material looks too big and coarse, and even where it doesn't it can alter the appearance of a building, making it look too bold. For example, much of the civil engineering work on Platt Lane uses Wills brickwork for 4 mm scale; it also has the correct English bond, which is not available in the 7 mm materials but is essential to represent Victorian civil engineering. I also find that the

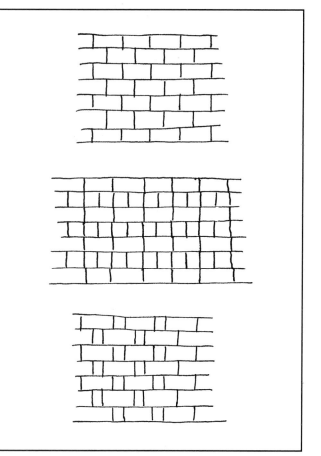

Different brick bonds. *Top* is stretcher bond, not often seen on traditional buildings, but used on modern ones; *middle* is Flemish bond, seldom seen in modern buildings, but once common; and *bottom* is English bond, the traditional style for civil engineering, including platforms, bridge piers, retaining walls, etc.

Left A rendered finish on a building, obtained by painting the plasticard wall with Sandtex from small sample tins, which is then coloured to suit. The building awaits detail such as drainpipes. *Andrew Booth*

Right Making windows

Below Sketch of the basic building shell as described in the text and shown in the photographs. Note that it is necessary to allow for the overlap of additional layers at the corners.

impression of the bond is more important than the size of the bricks, particularly on large expanses of wall, although I must admit that the additional number of courses, on platforms for example, may jar to some. Some walls are patched with different materials, for example brick in stone walls, particularly following the path of flues and chimneys. I'll talk a little more about the civil engineering later.

One finish that I find difficult to represent effectively is rendering. My preferred method to date is to create the shell as described, but to finish it smoothly, add any stone quoins or details and paint with Sandtex rendering paint, available in small sample tins. It dries to give a rough surface that I find particularly good. It can also be painted over. You must, however, ensure that any corner joints are clean and smooth, as any cracks and imperfections will show through. The accompanying sketches show how the corners and overlaps should be arranged to minimise any irregularities. Essentially, corners need to be overlapped to interlock with the next section when the walls are glued together. I make up walls separately, adding details such as courses, doorways, window frames (but not the doors and windows themselves) and details before final assembly on the shell.

Wooden planking, certainly in O gauge, I find is best made up plank by plank as shown in the sketches overleaf. Similarly I find it best to add corrugated iron sheet cladding sheet by sheet - at full size they are usually about 5 ft x 3 ft. I find the Slaters embossed material ideal for this.

Returning to the windows and doors, they are modelled next and attached to the plastic 'walls' before these are glued to the shell. A few sketches are

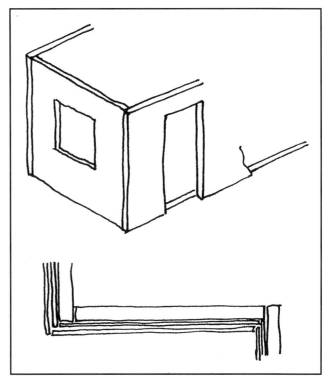

enclosed to show the principles. Basically, draw around the opening in the wall on a piece of 20 thou plasticard (for 7 mm scale), then cut out the opening. Usually the pencil line is slightly inside the aperture because of the thickness of the pencil; we can use this to our advantage to represent the frame! Next cut out the opening at this line, then make a second cut 5 mm outside the first so that this will fit into the aperture in the shell wall, which, you will remember, was 5 mm bigger all round than the finished window.

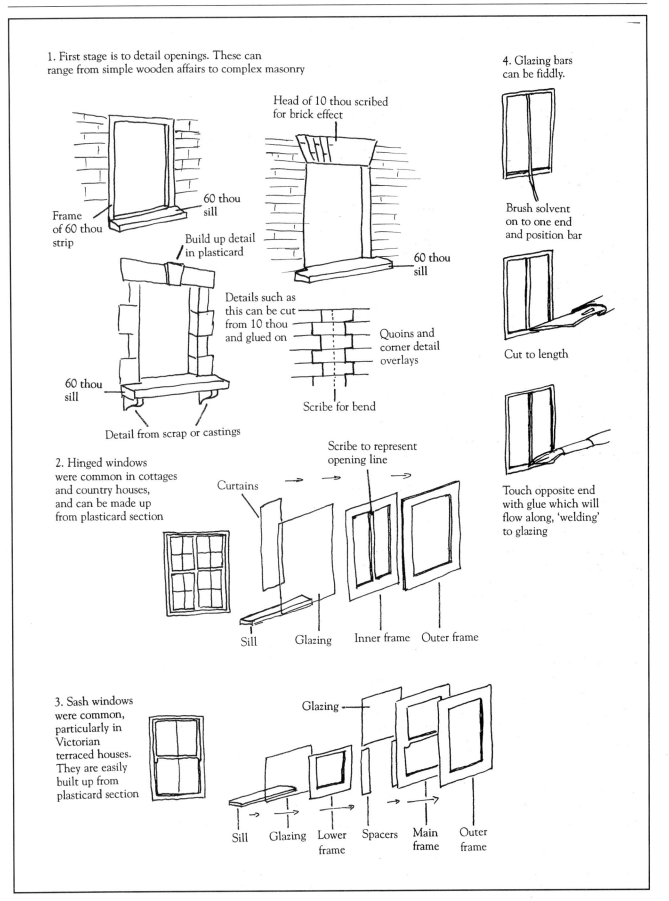

1. First stage is to detail openings. These can range from simple wooden affairs to complex masonry

Frame of 60 thou strip

60 thou sill

Head of 10 thou scribed for brick effect

60 thou sill

Build up detail in plasticard

Details such as this can be cut from 10 thou and glued on

Quoins and corner detail overlays

Scribe for bend

60 thou sill

Detail from scrap or castings

4. Glazing bars can be fiddly.

Brush solvent on to one end and position bar

Cut to length

Touch opposite end with glue which will flow along, 'welding' to glazing

2. Hinged windows were common in cottages and country houses, and can be made up from plasticard section

Curtains

Scribe to represent opening line

Sill   Glazing   Inner frame   Outer frame

3. Sash windows were common, particularly in Victorian terraced houses. They are easily built up from plasticard section

Glazing

Sill   Glazing   Lower frame   Spacers   Main frame   Outer frame

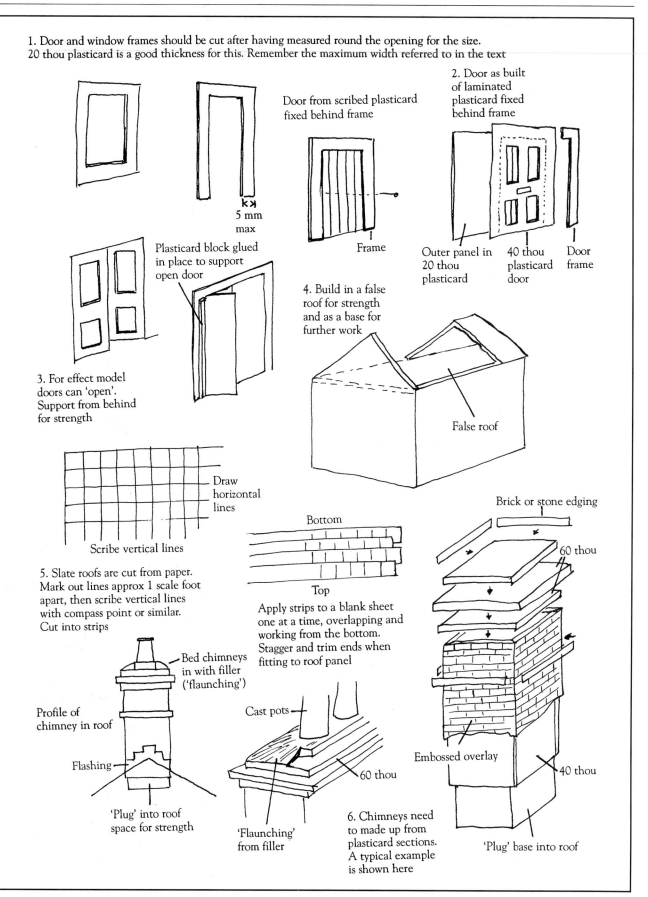

1. Door and window frames should be cut after having measured round the opening for the size. 20 thou plasticard is a good thickness for this. Remember the maximum width referred to in the text

5 mm max

Door from scribed plasticard fixed behind frame

Frame

2. Door as built of laminated plasticard fixed behind frame

Outer panel in 20 thou plasticard

40 thou plasticard door

Door frame

Plasticard block glued in place to support open door

3. For effect model doors can 'open'. Support from behind for strength

4. Build in a false roof for strength and as a base for further work

False roof

Draw horizontal lines

Scribe vertical lines

5. Slate roofs are cut from paper. Mark out lines approx 1 scale foot apart, then scribe vertical lines with compass point or similar. Cut into strips

Bottom

Top

Apply strips to a blank sheet one at a time, overlapping and working from the bottom. Stagger and trim ends when fitting to roof panel

Brick or stone edging

60 thou

Profile of chimney in roof

Bed chimneys in with filler ('flaunching')

Cast pots

Embossed overlay

40 thou

Flashing

'Plug' into roof space for strength

'Flaunching' from filler

60 thou

6. Chimneys need to made up from plasticard sections. A typical example is shown here

'Plug' base into roof

Left Doors, roofs and chimneys

Right a) To simulate lapped planking on a model start at the bottom and work upwards, overlapping the planks. Slope the bottom plank by adding a 1 mm strip at the bottom.

Flush planking (such as tongue-and-groove) can be represented by scribing, embossed sheet or by laying individual boards. Note that many boarded or wooden buildings have a masonry base.

Nice detail can be created by missing out odd boards, cutting out 'rotten' corners, etc.

b) For masonry buildings, quoins and plinths can be added from 10 and 20 thou plasticard. Thicker plinths can be built up as shown.

c) Corrugated iron panels for roofs and walls offer good opportunities for detail and weathering. Leave off the odd panel to reveal the wooden frame. Remember to fix the panels from the bottom up, overlapping as you go.

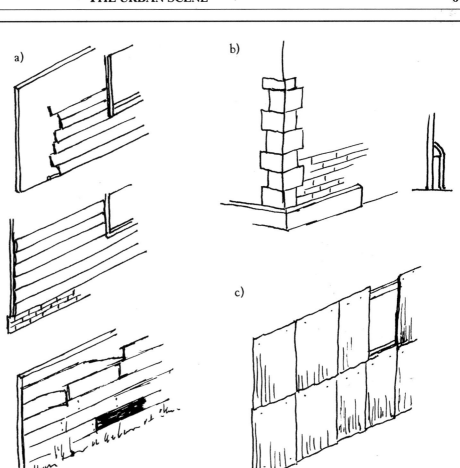

Essentially, windows and doors are built up from layers of plasticard (usually 20 thou is sufficient) and plastic glazing. Glazing bars and some of the finer detail is made from microstrip. Care needs to be taken not to damage the glazing material with solvent, so tack one end of the glazing bar in place by touching the end of a length of microstrip with solvent and putting it in place on the glazing. Allow to dry for a few seconds, then cut to length and touch the cut end with the solvent brush. The solvent will run along the length of the glazing bar, 'welding' it in place without the solvent running everywhere. This process can be continued, step by step, to build up some of the more complex patterns that can be seen. For smaller scales you may be able to take advantage of some of the ready-made etched and cast windows and doors available, and indeed use them for smaller windows in the larger scales.

Once the windows and doors are completed, they can be fixed in place behind the openings in the plastic walls. You may, of course, need to clean the apertures before the windows and doors can be fitted because they should be a close fit to the openings. You will also need to check before you fix them in place

whether they give the appearance of sufficiently thick walls - in other words, if they are sufficiently inset to give the impression of thick stone walls. If not, packing can be inserted between frame and wall.

When you are happy with the walls you can fix them in place on the shell with contact adhesive. The 40 thou 'intermediate' piece will now come into its own, protecting the detailed outer wall from any harmful effects from the contact adhesive. You may need to smooth the corners with fine abrasive paper and/or a little scraping - remember the old knife blades?

Pete and I have different approaches when it comes to modelling buildings clad in corrugated iron sheet. Peter prefers to build out from a shell of 4 mm clear polystyrene sheet using sheets of Slaters corrugated sheet material, which is quite thin and certainly could not be used without substantial support. Bolts are embossed on from the rear and sheets glued on individually, overlapped as appropriate. I prefer solid plasticard with the cladding applied as before. Where there is a window or, more commonly, a roof light - we'll deal with roofs in a minute - I cut a wider aperture than the finished one will be, and overlap it with the 'tin sheet'. For the simplest type microstrip can be used to represent the crude wooden frames often seen on farm buildings, whereas for 'proper' windows the same procedure is used as for windows in other types of walls. On, perhaps, an agricultural building, where often cladding has slipped to reveal a frame, I will represent this on a model by cutting a larger hole than necessary in the shell and using microstrip to represent the frame on which the cladding is fixed. The cladding is of course omitted, or fixed at an angle revealing the frame beneath.

The next stage in the process is to consider the roof. Roofs on model buildings are very important as they are often the most visible or obvious part of a building, yet they are often modelled quite shoddily, I suspect just to get a model finished! But before discussing the roof, it is worth mentioning at this stage the possibility of adding interior detail or lighting. It is easy to spend a lot of time on interior detail that cannot be seen, so if you are tempted to model an interior, restrict your activity to where it can be seen to the best advantage, and where the lighting can show off the interiors to good effect. For the next few paragraphs, however, let's assume no lighting or interiors.

The procedures for roofing the model are first to paint the bland white of the interior, second to fit a flat 'ceiling', third to build up the roof itself, and last to cover it with slates, tiles or whatever roofing material was used on the prototype. The interior should be painted black or dark grey; alternatively, black cartridge paper can be folded and positioned inside.

The roofing material most often seen on railway buildings is slate, so this seems to be a reasonable starting point. It is generally easier to work on a flat surface rather than a roof in situ on a model, so as with the walls, a flat sheet is cut and the roof covering built up on to it.

Two materials are commonly used to represent slates: plain typing paper or 10 thou plasticard. One has slightly more texture than the other - it's really a matter of personal preference which you use, and the procedure with both is the same. Most roofing slates are a smidgen under 12 inches wide; I don't think there was a standard size, but I may be wrong.

Whether you use paper or plastic, you will need to scribe lines a tad under a scale foot apart across the sheet, using a scribe - an empty fine-point biro is useful

Constructing slate roofs as described in the text. First the lines are ruled then the strips cut and glued on to the featherboard roof panel, each strip overlapping the previous one. The complete roof panel is then fixed to the building, in this case the terraced houses; note the cut-outs for chimneys, which are 'plugged' into the construction and glued to add strength to a vulnerable area. *P. Smith/Kirtley Models*

on paper, or a knife blade used sideways on plastic. A simple gadget that I have recently come across is a cutter sold under the trade name of 'OLFA'; it is a simple but very effective way both of cutting plastic and scoring for slate. (It also has a companion, the OLFA compass cutter, which is indispensable for cutting arches and curves in plastic.)

Next cut the sheets into strips a scale foot wide at right angles to the scored lines - one of the photos shows this process under way - having first marked one end so that all the strips are laid the same way round.

These strips are then stuck on to the plastic roof sheet mentioned earlier - contact adhesive for paper (being very careful not to get any on the surface), and Mek Pak for the plasticard. Work from the bottom of the roof upwards, making sure that the strips overlap as you go up. Once you have all the slates in place, trim your roof sheet to a final fit on the building and glue it in place with contact adhesive to featherboard, solvent to plastic.

You can add some detail in this process, perhaps cutting off an odd corner of a slate or cutting one out and moving it slightly out of line as if it has slipped. You can also add detail with a paintbrush, such as discoloration - but whatever you do with your tiles, be they chipped or slipped, don't overdo it or you will spoil the overall appearance. Again, it is a question of hinting rather than risking over-emphasis.

It may not have escaped your notice that I haven't suggested modelling or laying individual slates. This is partly because I am lazy, and partly because I don't see a sufficient advantage over the method just described. If it is your life's work to model a building as exactly as possible, then fine - but it ain't mine! I have tried it, but the results did not justify the extra time. Admittedly I have seen exquisite models with each slate and brick individually laid and painted, but I have also seen a lot more where this has been attempted and the effect has been rather less than convincing.

Tiled roofs can be modelled in a similar way, but the material used needs to be a little thicker. Pantiles were a devil to model until the arrival of the Wills Scenic sheets produced for 4 mm scale; I find they look perfect on 7 mm scale buildings as well. Corrugated iron roofs are modelled like walls of the same material mentioned earlier. Other types of roof such as stone flags or diminishing slate roofs require a variation on the original approach.

Detailing buildings

This is the stage when the imagination can run riot. You have a box that looks like a building, or at least it should do, and some of the basic details such as brick and roof slates, windows and doors. You can see it in your mind's eye, a perfect representation of brick down to the last stains, sagging gutters missing sections of downspout, perfectly straight chimney pots. The trick now is to make your little box fit that image, but before we move on to the details we need to consider adding the chimneys. I find these a pain in the proverbial to make; whether it is because at this late stage in the development of the model I am rushing for completion or not I don't know. I do know that this aspect is my *bête noire*. Chimneys and their detail are, however, a key and prominent part of a model, so you have no choice but to apply a little care and attention to their construction. Model a chimney well and it will go unnoticed, part of the scene - model it badly and it will stick out like a sore thumb!

I included a sketch on page 60 showing the general arrangements for constructing chimneys. Virtually any type of chimney can be built using this basic method. Keeping them upright and square, and giving them some strength - they are after all in a vulnerable spot - is an important consideration. The 'plug' at the bottom should be long enough to glue right into the hole that you have cut into the roof, to locate it. Any *slight* discrepancies can be covered with a representation of lead flashing, but be careful, because if you get it wrong you will need a new roof panel.

Chimney pots come in a variety of styles, and usually a suitable selection of cast ones can be obtained from Scalelink, S&D and Springside, to name but three. These need to be bedded into filler, which represents cement and holds them in place. Lead flashing can be added - 10 thou plasticard is suitable for 7 mm scale; alternatively masking-tape or modelling clay can be used. If you are modelling from the mid-1950s onward, you might consider TV aerials, but don't forget that there weren't that many until the 1960s, so don't overdo it, and don't forget that the style changed from the VHF to UHF type. These can easily be modelled with a bit of wire, but they need to be modelled carefully and shouldn't stand out; like much detailing they are better omitted than becoming too obvious through bad modelling.

Before a paintbrush is let anywhere near the model, bargeboards, gutters and downpipes need to be added. Cast and moulded examples are readily available, and the better ones provide a good representation of some of the older, more ornate styles. These 'rainwater goods', as I believe they are collectively known, are supplemented, certainly in O gauge, by cast boxes and brackets. I find it difficult with some of the cast ones sold in short lengths to get a straight line, and a great deal of care is necessary to get them to look right - it is, however, often worth the effort.

To save cost and to make matters a bit easier, unless you want the specific type available as castings, you can make your own quite easily, either from plastic strip as shown in the diagram opposite, or by using metal or plastic channel of a suitable section. Downspouts are simply made with suitable round material, such as plastic rod or brass tube - about 3 mm outside diameter seems about right for 7 mm. Details can be simply added to bare pipes and section to represent brackets, etc.

I mentioned bargeboards earlier. These help to finish a model by giving an edging to the roof, although of course on real buildings they have a specific purpose and are not merely for decoration. However careful I am at trying to measure off these during construction, I never get them right. I have now learned to cheat and hold a sheet of plasticard of appropriate thickness (40 thou is generally useful for 7 mm scale) against the gable end of the building and draw along the roof

to get the exact angle - mark below this line to the depth of board you require and allow for any extensions. Some boards are quite well detailed with shaped edges or piercing - I am afraid there is little alternative to trying to copy this on the model in the larger scales. I avoid any bargeboards with cut-outs, but simple shaped edges can normally be reproduced quite straightforwardly with a good sharp scalpel, having first pencilled on the pattern.

Mention of finishing gable ends reminds me that the roof will also require finishing with the addition of ridge tiles. Most types of ridge tiles can be easily represented from simple materials as shown in the sketches. The more ornate ones can often be modelled using specific etchings or mouldings that are available; alternatively, other shaped materials, such as valancing for station canopies, can, suitably cut down, be pressed into use.

Now is the time to consider adding a bit of colour to your creation. But before you dash off for brush and paint, pause a while. If you have gone to a lot of trouble to get the building to represent your chosen style, what about the colour? Colour plays a very important part in giving the overall impression, so a little time spent on selecting it is worthwhile. I don't know for sure whether I have a bee in my bonnet about it, but brickwork, and stone for that matter, takes on its own distinctive colour, which is a product of its source and location - for example, the clays that made the brick and the effects of the weather and atmosphere, and where the structures are. In short, you therefore need to know what colour your model *should* be, rather than just painting it generic stone or brick colours. You also need to consider whether your structures

Above left and left The terraced houses with detail in place, and in their finished, painted condition. The drainpipes are 3 mm brass tube held in place with split pins, while detailed castings for the soil pipe, roof cappings and chimney pots have also been added. *Author*

Right Detailing model buildings

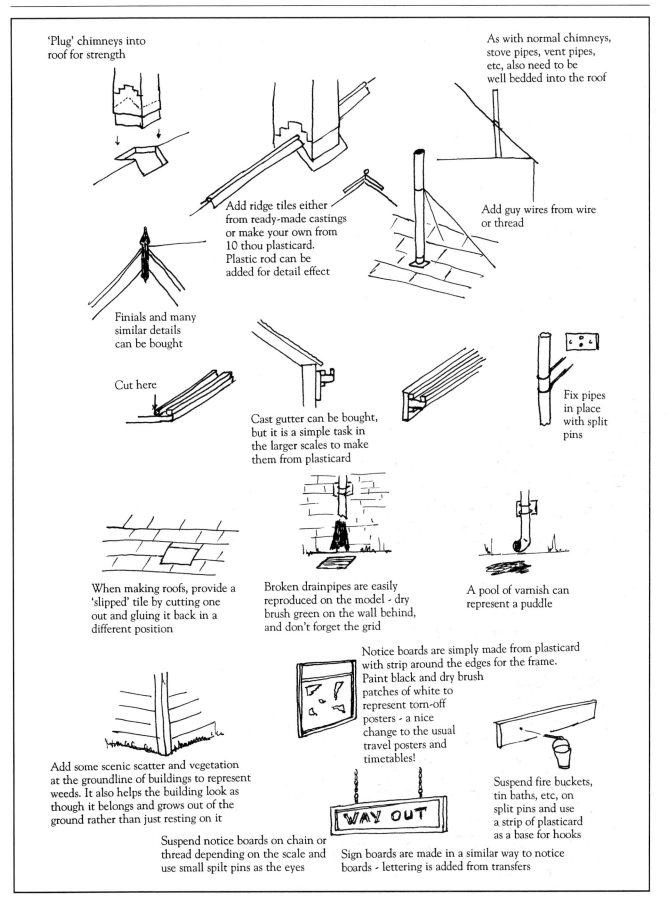

'Plug' chimneys into roof for strength

As with normal chimneys, stove pipes, vent pipes, etc, also need to be well bedded into the roof

Add ridge tiles either from ready-made castings or make your own from 10 thou plasticard. Plastic rod can be added for detail effect

Add guy wires from wire or thread

Finials and many similar details can be bought

Cut here

Cast gutter can be bought, but it is a simple task in the larger scales to make them from plasticard

Fix pipes in place with split pins

When making roofs, provide a 'slipped' tile by cutting one out and gluing it back in a different position

Broken drainpipes are easily reproduced on the model - dry brush green on the wall behind, and don't forget the grid

A pool of varnish can represent a puddle

Add some scenic scatter and vegetation at the groundline of buildings to represent weeds. It also helps the building look as though it belongs and grows out of the ground rather than just resting on it

Notice boards are simply made from plasticard with strip around the edges for the frame. Paint black and dry brush patches of white to represent torn-off posters - a nice change to the usual travel posters and timetables!

Suspend fire buckets, tin baths, etc, on split pins and use a strip of plasticard as a base for hooks

Suspend notice boards on chain or thread depending on the scale and use small spilt pins as the eyes

WAY OUT

Sign boards are made in a similar way to notice boards - lettering is added from transfers

have a particular type of brick, for example engineers blue brick or Accrington brick, which require a surface with just the merest hint of sheen.

The next few sentences describe the approach taken when embossed plastic sheet is used. Strange though it may seem, the first area to be coloured is the mortar joints. No, you don't try and paint the fine recessed line in the sheet. If that were possible - I'm sure someone somewhere has done it - it would be mind-blowingly tedious and take hours. What you do is cheat. You take a diluted mix of a suitable colour and wash it over the brick or stonework and leave it overnight to dry. One point to note, though - make sure you stir your paint thoroughly before you take some from the tin and dilute it. If you don't you may find the wash dries glossy, and I've never seen shiny mortar! You will find that the walls look a bit messy and you may be a little appalled at the appearance, but take heart. This process will have left the recessed mortar course filled with this colour, while the bricks or stones are comparatively free of colour.

It is these that the next stage tackles, and there are a number of ways to proceed. I have used them all and I think you may wish to try one or two alternatives; indeed, you may develop variations to suit your way of working. So long as you end up with realistically coloured brick and stone, how you get it matters not a jot.

Method 1 Take a large artist's brush - the stiff-bristle type sold for oils - and dry brush over the brickwork with enamel paint mixed to a suitable overall colour (preferably a bit lighter in tone than you think you'll need - I'll explain why later). Make sure the paint is matt and well stirred. Once you have got your basic wash in place, vary the colour slightly and just gently dry brush a few odd bricks here and there in a little grouping; perhaps even pick out the odd individual brick. Also dry brush on other detail such as green for moss stains under gutters and behind drain pipes, black for sooty deposits on bridge arches, etc.

Method 2 Proceed as above, but let the base colour you apply on the brick dry thoroughly. Then take a selection of two or three suitable artist's pastels of the chalk type that can be bought in individual sticks from artists' shops, and rub them, sideways on, over the brick. Vary your colours, and over-colour some bits as you did before with the paints to give the effect you want. I quite like this method as it is quick and you are ensured of a matt finish and a little bit of texture to boot! Pencil crayons can also be used, but I find them a bit fiddly.

For engineers blue brick I find a very good effect is obtained by spraying the walls with a medium to dark grey car spray, then rubbing a dark purple, navy blue and grey pastel over the basic grey. As the mortar used in this type of wall is usually grey, I don't bother with the mortar wash except perhaps to show a bit of later pointing or patching, when a tiny amount of diluted wash can be applied and allowed to run into the mortar courses.

Surprisingly I haven't found it necessary to fix the colour, but I suppose you could spray it with varnish, first of course masking any glass that should remain glossy.

Method 3 After the colouring of the mortar course has been applied, the brick is treated with crayons or pastels and a varied colour effect created. The walls are then dry brushed with a deep red, say vermilion, which gives an elusive warm colour and helps blend everything in.

All three variations were used on the Platt Lane project, and I think there are two golden rules to bear in mind.

One: don't be too fussy and try to go for too much detail such as trying to paint each brick individually. Remember that we are trying to create an impression, that the buildings are part of a bigger scene and that too much detail and too strong a colour won't look right. Take a look at a building, or at least a whole elevation. At a distance you will see an overall picture, colours and hues, not a lot of individual detail, although some odd bits may just show up a little more.

Two: don't paint the building in too strong a block of colour. Tone down the colours by adding a little grey or off-white, particularly on buildings at the back of the layout, to help create an illusion of distance. It has to be remembered that colour doesn't usually follow the same scale reduction as basic dimensions. If you had, for example, the exact colour something was painted and applied it to a 1.43 or 1.76 scale model, the size of the object would have been reduced but not the colour! Suitable hints of colour are better than solid blocks. Remember also that objects made of natural substances such as brick or stone are not of uniform colour by the very nature of their origins.

The above notes have primarily related to brick, and while I have hinted at stone, a few words on that material are necessary.

Mortar courses aren't usually as obvious as they are on a brick wall and generally you don't need to worry about trying to paint them. A suitable base colour is applied by dry brushing over the embossed stone, and individual stones (being much bigger than bricks this is much easier) are picked out basically using the methods described for brick except that it is usually

The final painting and finishing of any model is an opportunity to add a further dimension, and breathe a little life into it. Here even the simplest of 4 mm scale plastic kits has been painted and dry-brushed as described in the text to bring out the textures of the stone in the foreground shed, and to add detail to the building at the rear where the effect of water from a leaking downspout has been painted on to the brickwork. The stone setts have been painted and washes allowed to flow into the gaps between the moulded stones to good effect. *Author*

While painting can add a new dimension to a good model, it can also spoil it, and sometimes it is preferable to understate the effect required, as in this example. Note the different materials used to make up the exterior walls, something easily achieved with the methods described. The ivy growing up the corner of the building is Woodland Scenics foliage mat. *P. Smith/Kirtley Models*

sufficient merely to vary the basic colour, slightly lightening or darkening it.

Wooden or corrugated sheet walls simply require painting with perhaps a bit of dry brushing to show discolouration or rust. Even though you may use gloss paint on the full-size woodwork on your house, use matt on the model - as with colour, glossiness does not transfer down to model size, and a gloss wall on a model building would look, frankly, ridiculous.

Painting the roof follows a similar process. First paint it a basic overall colour, then follow this with dry brushing downwards from the ridge. For a slate or tiled roof you can pick out the odd slate in a slight variation of the base colour. I emphasise 'slight' and 'odd', otherwise your roof will look like a patchwork quilt rather than a roof that has been in place with the same tiles and through the same weather and pollution since the building was constructed. Pantiles generally only require a very diluted wash with dark grey, and perhaps the odd bit of dry brushing to represent moss or other patches of discoloration.

At this stage, with the roof and walls painted, the rest of the building can be painted, and I would suggest next moving to the window frames - many buildings have white frames and therefore you might be able to avoid having to paint them. Where you do have to paint them be careful - a fine good-quality brush and patience are required. If you do get paint on the clear plastic glass, use a clean brush and white spirit to remove it before it dries. Also paint doors, bargeboards, gutters and downspouts; you can slip a piece of thin paper behind the drainpipes to help avoid getting paint on the brick or stonework.

I have already mentioned using a paintbrush to add a little detail, and there are a number of other opportunities to develop this when our model building reaches this stage. For example, rust streaks from ironwork, moss and damp patches, bird droppings - but as always subtlety and understatement are necessary. Don't overdo it. Other details can be added such as door handles made from pins, sign boards, enamel signs and fire buckets, which are often available from the model trade and, carefully added, are an effective way of breathing a bit of life into a model (see page 65).

When it comes to actually placing the finished building on the layout, don't just plonk it down and leave it. Buildings grow from foundations laid in the

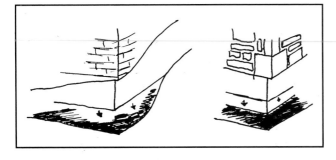

'Plugging' buildings into 'sockets' so that they appear to grow from the ground rather than just sit on top of it.

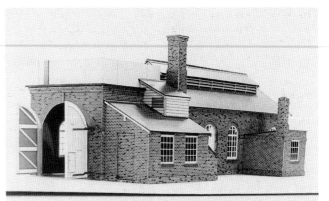

A 4 mm scale engine shed built from a card kit as bought, with no added detail. *Author's collection*

ground. If you just place your model down, you will get a tell-tale black line around the base and, if the site or the building's base isn't perfectly flat, you may get a bigger gap in some places. Obviously real buildings have neither black lines nor gaps, so we need to make sure they are effectively bedded into the layout. Footpaths, roadways and weeds often do the trick. Where buildings are known to be going on an uneven site, it is usually easier to make the walls of the shell (but not the detail) longer than absolutely necessary to form a 'plug' that can either fit into a 'socket' in the scenic base, or have the ground contoured up to the bottom of the exterior walls. The sketches above should clarify this.

Before leaving the subject of buildings I think a few thoughts on putting together and improving plastic building kits is necessary. If you model in the smaller scales you are comparatively well served with kits for railway buildings and structures in plastic and, to a lesser extent, card. Some of these kits are excellent products, which with a little care in construction and finishing really do provide a fine model.

With plastic kits I generally find it better to paint and glaze doors and windows while they are still on

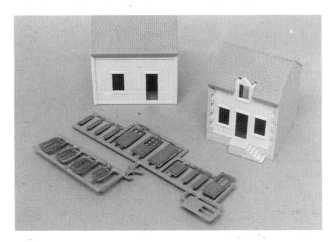

Early stages in the construction of a plastic kit, showing the technique of painting windows, doors, etc, while the parts are still on the sprue. *Author*

their sprue. Sometimes it is possible to 'tack' the roof in place to help keep the building square until the walls are set.

Plastic kits lend themselves to 'bashing', ie chopping them about and making different buildings from the parts supplied. As with scratch-building, detailing and painting with attention to detail makes all the difference.

Ever since primary school, and attempts at making fold-and-glue comb-cases, I have had an aversion to modelling in card. This is not to say that excellent results cannot be obtained from card models, but just that the material is not my cup of tea.

There are many good-quality pre-colored card kits available that make up into very passable models. But there are some simple ways to improve them. First, a sharp hard pencil ruled along the mortar lines gives some relief to the otherwise flat card. Planking can be similarly scored, but I prefer where possible to replace it with embossed or home-made plastic planking. Second, the colours can be weathered with dry brushing using water colours - but be careful, as it is easy to destroy the colouring and damage the card! Third, while some kits now provide plastic detail components, those that don't will benefit from the addition of cast, moulded or etched details such as chimney pots, valances, doors, etc. The key to successful card kits is a sharp knife with which to cut the components cleanly. Have plenty of spare blades to hand - and patience!

Civil engineering

The Platt Lane project layout has a lot of what I would call 'civil engineering' - bridges, retaining walls and the like. While these are clearly an integral part of the design of the layout and are basically masonry structures, their representation in model form is worth a brief mention.

The Platt Lane coal drops under construction. The importance of the design of the baseboard in providing the base for such civil engineering is clear. Also seen is the balsa strip that provides the basis for the stone capping.

The provision of rails across bridges, piers or, as in this case, coal drops requires a different approach. Normally cast chairs are used in these situations, but they are usually fitted to longitudinal timber or steel sections (often with a timber runner) running between piers or abutments to span the drops. I used readily available chairs slid along rail sections and glued down to balsa strips representing the longitudinal timbers. The ends of the chairs needed trimming with a sharp knife to prevent their overhanging the balsa, and of course needed to be spaced as for ordinary track - easily done using a spare length as a template when gluing them in place. *Author*

Retaining walls are, as their name suggests, designed to retain earthworks in their intended form. Because railway engineers endeavour to keep railways as level as possible with changes in level as gradual as possible, inevitably you can't move far without encountering earthworks and quite commonly some form of retaining wall. They may be of brick, stone or concrete, vertical or sloped, and containing arches or buttresses; at their very simplest they comprise shuttering made from old sleepers preventing soil from spilling on to the track.

Modelling retaining walls, bridge piers, etc, is a simple and straightforward operation if you make provision for them at the planning and design stage and in the design and construction of the baseboards. I have included some photographs of the construction of the retaining walls and bridge piers on Platt Lane, and drawings showing how variations in the 'plain wall' type can be built - arches, slopes, safety refuges, etc.

The coal drops are another variation on the basic theme and I have similarly included a photograph showing the general arrangement.

Most brickwork used for civil engineering work on the railways was constructed in English bond (see page 57), and this brick is I believe visually quite noticeably different from the Flemish or stretcher bond commonly used for other structures. All the common brick bonds are available in the various 4 mm scale embossed and moulded brickwork sheets on the market. In 2 mm scale the situation is similar, and for both there are also ready-made sections of walls and platforms available. However, in 7 mm scale there is to my knowledge at

A typical stone-built retaining wall - note that the wall is not sloped but vertical and there are no buttresses. The courses of smaller stones in the top section are an important detail. Bolton Trinity Street, April 1960. *D. Hampson*

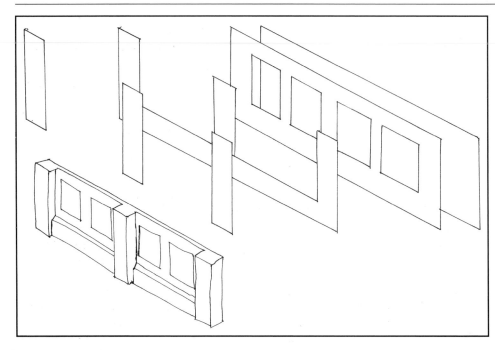

Left In the heyday of railway building, bricklayers enjoyed showing off their art, and many decorative types of walling were designed around their function. The type of wall shown here was common in an urban setting, and the LNWR was a big user of the type for platform walls and the like. They are relatively easy to model using laminates of plasticard to build up the design of panels, recesses and piers.

Left The retaining walls on Platt Lane, of which there are a great many, are vertical brick with no buttresses. The baseboard construction provides the frame on which the detail is added in the form of moulded plastic brickwork. Here we see the arrangement of the walls adjacent to the underbridge, the boundary wall to the coal yard and the stone sett sheets in place. The flat wall cappings are plasticard, while the pier capping is carved from balsa wood. The bridge piers are made from the same moulded brick sheets, but their corners need to be chamfered to get a good fit; this is something best achieved by using a large flat file! The joins between the moulded brick sheets show less in the flesh than in the picture; some will be disguised by pipes, while an advertising hoarding will stand over the boundary wall. The brickwork is carried right through the underpass and will be painted white. *Author*

Left A wider view of the finished area showing how the civil engineering is coming together (also showing, incidentally, the cinema in place). *Author*

the time of writing no material available to represent the correct English bond. Accordingly you have a choice of either using what is available, though strictly incorrect, or scribing your own!

I have mentioned from time to time the use in 7 mm scale of products intended for smaller scales, and I actually used 4 mm English bond brickwork sheets for the retaining walls and bridge piers on Platt Lane. The reason for this was twofold. I wanted to create an illusion of greater height and delicacy of the brick walls supporting the railway and the associated piers, but at the same time, because they featured so prominently, to avoid them swamping the layout visually. There is also of course the advantage of being able to use correct English bond brickwork. The material used comes from the Wills Scenic range, and an awful lot of it was used.

The only problem, if indeed it can be so described, is where this walling meets up with the walling at the side and rear of the station building. I debated various means of hiding or disguising this joint, but in the end decided to make it obvious. The bridge support and retaining walls are painted to represent engineers blue brick - commonly used for this type of work - whereas the station itself is in red brick; the former is Wills 4 mm English bond, the latter Slaters 7 mm scale Flemish bond! Making the distinction so obvious seems to prevent the eye dwelling on the difference and actively being drawn to seek out the disguise!

The walling and bridge supports are simple, basic affairs, vertical walls, no fancy arches or brickwork, merely stone stretchers and capping added later. This, while typical of this type of structure, is of course not what appeared at Great Moor Street itself, our source for the model.

Unlike red brick, I find that mortar courses in structures made of engineers blue brick are not so obvious, and this makes painting somewhat easier. For the work on Platt Lane the sheets of brickwork were applied to the substructure, then the 40 thou plastic strips representing the stone stretchers were applied and the whole lot sprayed with a dark grey car touch-up colour, BL Hurricane Grey. This, with the orange red of the plastic brickwork, produced a purple/blue tint and formed an ideal base for further colouring. This I achieved with a selection of two or three suitably coloured soft pastels of the chalk type that were rubbed, flat side down, across the brickwork until the desired colour and finish was achieved. The strips of plasticard applied to represent the stone were simply painted a matt dark grey enamel. The bridge piers were treated similarly and the stone bands carried underneath the bridge. The only difference was that the brickwork under the bridge was sprayed matt white enamel to represent the white glazed brickwork commonly found in this situation.

The basic materials for the pier and wall cappings are plasticard strips or balsa - if you wanted a real 'Rolls-Royce' job you could carve your own from modelling clay or a similar material. Many walls, particularly in urban settings, were topped with iron rail fencing. Railway companies cast their own stanchions and often old tubing was used for rails. This can be represented in model form quite easily using turned brass or moulded plastic stanchions sold for model boat handrails, which are available in a variety of sizes; a cheaper alternative is to use split pins. In either case piano wire or brass rod can be used for the rails.

The other remaining bit of civil engineering on Platt Lane is the coal drops, already mentioned, and these were illustrated in *Baseboard Basics and Making Tracks*, the first book in the series. The original LNWR drawings on which they were based did not reflect exactly what was actually built; the drops at Platt Lane were somewhat simplified, particularly in relation to the brickwork on the supporting piers - this I believe reflected more what was actually done rather than planned.

This typical LNWR-style plate girder bridge stood almost at the platform ends of Great Moor Street, and provided the base of the model bridge. The background of the plates was maroon, the lettering white, achieved on the model with transfers of very similar though not quite exact lettering. *D. Hampson*

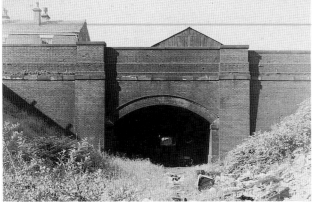

Above left and right These two pictures showing the variety of bridges on the lines out of Great Moor Street are included to show what bridges actually look like rather than how we imagine them to be; they also show that the style and building materials used can change within a very short distance. *D. Hampson*

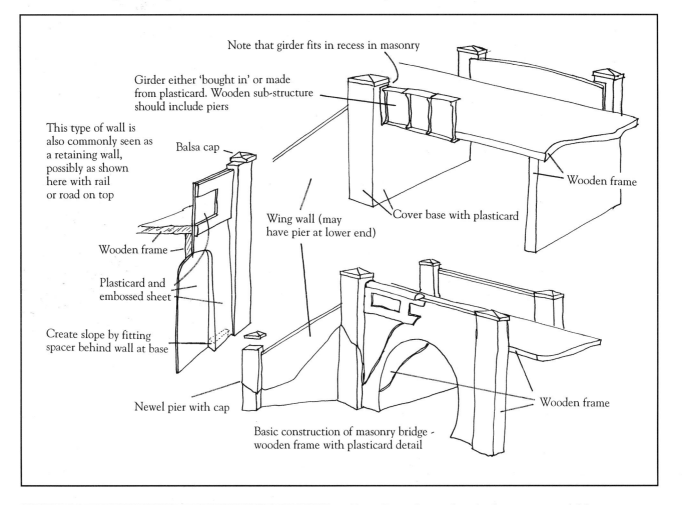

Note that girder fits in recess in masonry

Girder either 'bought in' or made from plasticard. Wooden sub-structure should include piers

This type of wall is also commonly seen as a retaining wall, possibly as shown here with rail or road on top

Balsa cap

Wooden frame

Cover base with plasticard

Wing wall (may have pier at lower end)

Wooden frame

Plasticard and embossed sheet

Create slope by fitting spacer behind wall at base

Newel pier with cap

Wooden frame

Basic construction of masonry bridge - wooden frame with plasticard detail

Above Reproducing these bridge types in model form.

Left Detail showing the arrangement of stone piers with an iron plate girder bridge; this one is at Entwistle. *Author*

Right and middle right Different types of platform surfacing at a forlorn-looking Great Moor Street. The nearest platform has concrete paving laid conventionally, reproduced on the platform concourse at Platt Lane. *D. Hampson; Author*

Bottom left The far platform is surfaced with Staffordshire blue paving tiles, of which the LNWR was a great user. This was the original platform surface, and I have finished one platform of Platt Lane in this style, using embossed plasticard intended to represent chequer plate! Whilst not entirely accurate, it does look quite effective when sprayed grey and detailed with coloured chalk pastels as described in the text for the retaining walls. The bracket starter signal is interesting. *D. Hampson*

Bottom right Stone setts are the surface of this loading bank at Great Moor Street. Note also the railings at the edge the dock of the type described in the text.

Although the station closed to passengers in 1954 it was used for summer excursion and holiday traffic for several seasons afterwards, mostly for services to North Wales. One of the few reliefs from the monotony of local passenger and freight workings for local Plodder Lane shed men was a trip on a Patricroft 'Precursor' to Wales. *D. Hampson*

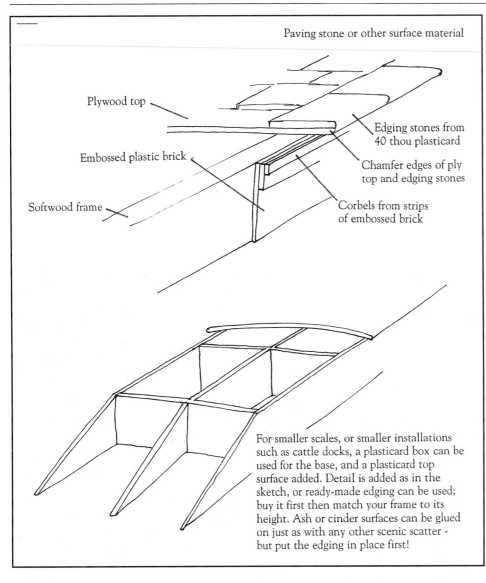

Paving stone or other surface material

Plywood top

Embossed plastic brick

Softwood frame

Edging stones from 40 thou plasticard

Chamfer edges of ply top and edging stones

Corbels from strips of embossed brick

For smaller scales, or smaller installations such as cattle docks, a plasticard box can be used for the base, and a plasticard top surface added. Detail is added as in the sketch, or ready-made edging can be used; buy it first then match your frame to its height. Ash or cinder surfaces can be glued on just as with any other scenic scatter - but put the edging in place first!

Left Sketch showing how the detail was built up for Platt Lane's platforms.

Below The construction of the Platt Lane platforms with brick facing including corbels, plywood surface and stone flag mouldings in place. *Author*

Bottom An alternative type of platform surfacing under construction. Embossed plastic sheet intended for chequer plating has been used to represent Staffordshire blue tiles. The plywood top edging is visible, and requires smoothing to shape. The brick corbels can just be seen beneath the ply. *Author*

Below Stone paving in model form on the far platform at Platt Lane. *Author*

4.
SIGNALLING

I thought long and hard as to whether signalling should be covered in a volume on scenic modelling rather than in the first volume, which covered the mechanical aspects of the model railway. However, on the basis that signalling has a high visual impact and certainly affects the appearance of a model railway, I have included it here.

Signalling is quite a complex subject on its own and there a numerous books and articles on this aspect of railways, real and model. I think, however, that it is necessary in this volume to outline very basically the prototype practice on semaphore signalling before we look at signalling on the model.

Let me say at the outset that it is perfectly possible to adopt a minimalist approach to model railway signalling, but to do so you have to choose a prototype that adopted this; on the standard gauge at least, in so far as mainland Britain is concerned, this means a light railway. If you are modelling the Euston approaches you can't really get away with one signal!

These notes relate first to practices by the main railway companies in Britain on a general basis, and second do not take into account specific practices or idiosyncrasies evolved by individual railways, particularly significant before the 1923 'Grouping'.

On the real railway signals are the link between the mobile - footplate - and stationary - station and operating - sides of the railway; indeed, the only effective communication. Lamp codes were also an integral part of this communication network, but for our present purpose it is merely sufficient to acknowledge their existence along with the telegraph bell codes that communicated information along the railway system between signal boxes, anticipating and reporting train movements and warning of the need for action.

Signals are primarily there to control the movement of trains. Railways are divided into 'blocks' or sections into which, in general, only one train is allowed at a time. (However, because each train is under the control of its own crew it is feasible to allow more than one train into a section at one time in certain conditions - the 'permissive block'.)

The resulting 'block system' has each block provided with a signal box located within it, with entry to the next block section controlled by a Home, or stop, signal. This signal is kept 'on' (at Danger) until the section ahead is declared clear by the signalman in charge of it, and the train can then proceed. Clearly it takes some time to stop a train travelling at speed, so a Distant or warning signal appears before the Home signal to protect it and give advance warning of both its presence and its position. The Distant in the 'on' position does not indicate stop, but warns that the approaching Home signal is so positioned; similarly, the Distant in the 'off' position indicates that the Home is also off, and the line is clear into the next block section ahead. I have enclosed a sketch overleaf showing how this applies.

The sketch also shows how it applies where there is a station in the section. The usual practice was to end a block at the start of the platform, but place a further Home signal, known as the Starter, beyond the other end of the platform to allow another train to enter the platform when the preceding one had moved into the section ahead.

In the era of our project layout, most stations, indeed all but the smallest, usually had some sidings or modest goods facility that was shunted by the pick-up goods train. This area and the need to access and shunt it required further protection, and this could be achieved by including two further Home signals, an Inner Home and Advance Starter; again, the arrangement is sketched.

As a result of the limited distances that mechanical signalling and, more importantly, point control rodding could cover, a pair of linked signal boxes often controlled larger stations. In addition, subsidiary controls - ground frames - might be provided to control

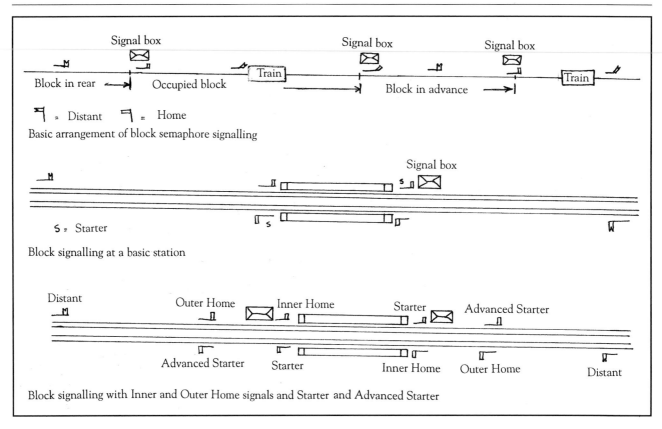

Signal box · Signal box · Signal box

Block in rear ← → Occupied block · Train · Block in advance →

⌐ = Distant   ⌐ = Home

Basic arrangement of block semaphore signalling

Signal box

S = Starter

Block signalling at a basic station

Distant · Outer Home · Inner Home · Starter · Advanced Starter

Advanced Starter · Starter · Inner Home · Outer Home · Distant

Block signalling with Inner and Outer Home signals and Starter and Advanced Starter

Types of semaphore block signalling.

sidings or yards. The important point about this is that while the area of station and yard is part of the block system, in order to achieve flexibility it is not constrained by the requirements of the rest of the block system.

In many instances, as in termini or concentrated areas of railway, block sections were short and it was necessary to place the Distant signal operated by one box on the same post as the Starter of the previous section. Each arm was controlled by a separate box, so they were interlocked mechanically in order that the Distant could not be 'off' when the Home above it was 'on'; both could of course be 'on' or 'off' at the same time, or the Home 'off' but the Distant displaying caution, warning that the next Home would be at Danger.

Junctions were normally controlled by bracket signals or gantries, and the arrangement of a double-track junction is shown in the sketch on page 78. Where both routes could be taken at speed a 'splitting Distant' was used giving warning for both routes; again, these may be on the same post as a preceding Home arm.

Bracket signals were also used to control access across other 'facing' points into loops or other running lines and sidings. Larger installations usually called for gantries, but an alternative, quite commonly used by the GWR, was to include illuminated route

Model LNWR signals of the type to be used at Platt Lane. Those on the right are underslung; note the detail of lamps and spectacles on those on the right. *John Matthews*

Below Perhaps the best way to operate model railway signals is by the use of solenoids beneath the baseboard, but prototype operating wires and pulleys can be modelled using thread or fine wire fixed to posts approximately 6 feet apart; don't have the wires too taut. In the smaller scales it would be sufficient to glue the wire to the post; in O gauge and above a pinhead protruding from a balsa post would simulate a pulley.

Point-operating rods are usually inverted 'U'-section steel running on rollers. Castings for these and associated cranks are available in 4 and 7 mm scales; the rod can be made from square-section plastic or brass rod.

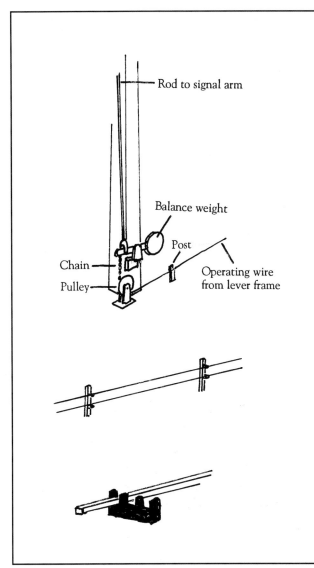

Above In the right foreground can be seen how signal wires and point rodding are brought down and turned under the track where necessary, by means of pulley-wheels and cranks respectively. Faded wooden signs like the one shown were common - indeed, all the paraphernalia seen on and against the wall would be a fascinating challenge to the modeller! Eric Blakey collection/L&YR Society

Above Single-track lines were usually operated with the aid of the 'staff' or 'token' system. Only one staff at a time could be withdrawn from electrically interlocked machines at each end of the single line; the driver, collecting such an instrument from the signalman, was thus permitted to proceed down the line, giving up the staff at the other end, where it was replaced in the machine, clearing the section. Here the driver of ex-LSWR 'O2' tank No 16 Ventnor is receiving the token for the Smallbrook-Brading section at Smallbrook Junction on the Isle of Wight. Author's collection

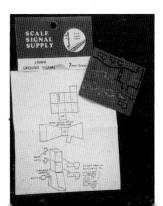

Right A typical kit for a 7 mm scale ground signal. Author

Left An LNWR junction bracket signal with LMS upper quadrant arms fitted, still fulfilling its original role in the early 1960s. Note that the arm for the left-hand route has a Distant arm below the Home, indicating that the next stop signal is not far round the curve. Note also the filthy wooden posts, not repainted for many years, and the guy ropes. *D. Hampson*

Below Semaphore signalling at a double-track junction

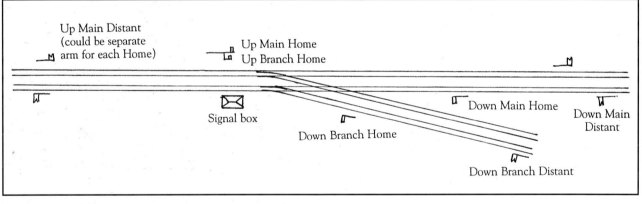

indicator below a single arm that cleared for each route.

'Calling-on' arms, smaller than and placed below the main arms, were used to permit a driver to advance past a Home signal at Danger; one was commonly provided on terminal roads to allow a locomotive to enter a road already occupied, perhaps to draw away stock. Calling-on arms are not usually found on the archetypal single-track branch.

Other special signal arms were also used. The 'shunt ahead' signal permitted trains to draw forward a certain distance into the section in advance; the 'backing' signal governed the reversal into a siding; and siding or 'ground' signals, often comprising small arms or discs, permitted a train to leave a siding or make another internal shunting movement. There were many versions of these latter signals, the railway companies having their own styles which perhaps varied more than those of the main arms. Despite the description, they were not always restricted to location on the ground and could be seen on gantries and brackets. Perhaps their most common application for modellers is the control of the release crossover in stations. Those interested are advised to consult one of the appropriate excellent signalling books available.

I am conscious that this is the merest outline of practice, and does not reflect local or company policy and practice, nor modern 'colour light' signalling, let alone the very different principles of signalling elsewhere, such as France or Germany. Of more importance to

the modeller, however, is the need to note that signalling and signal boxes are long lived. Indeed, many original boxes from the last century, albeit suitably modified, are still in use on our main lines and basically the same as when built. Signals also lasted well and many still survive with little modification, save from the change to upper quadrant or more modern arms.

Signals are not too common on model railways, and if you've ever tried to make them you will probably understand why! However, as I said at the outset of this chapter, I think they are essential to the visual appearance and character of the model railway layout and the picture we are trying to portray.

Fortunately there are a number of good kits and partly

Below Not the best quality, but an interesting photograph in that it shows the signalling for departures at Great Moor Street. The arrangement is similar to that adopted for Platt Lane, which has little open line between platform end and fiddle yard, certainly far too little to do much about signalling the approach. The manual lever between the tracks to operate the loco release crossover is unusual. *D. Hampson*

Above A GWR ground disc signal in the 'off' position, allowing exit from the siding on to the main line. *Author's collection*

Below right The Platt Lane signalling diagram, which has been prepared in accordance with the anticipated movements within the confines of the model, and not the totality of possibilities, which would require a forest of signals! Instead it represents the minimum requirement having regard for LNWR/LMS/BR practice. It is assumed that the signals controlling the approach to the station are 'offstage'.

The 'yellow' ground signals can be passed at Danger to allow shunting within the confines of their appropriate sidings, but must be cleared to allow access on to the main line. 'F' stands for facing point lock, an important necessity on the prototype to prevent point blades from moving or being moved beneath trains.

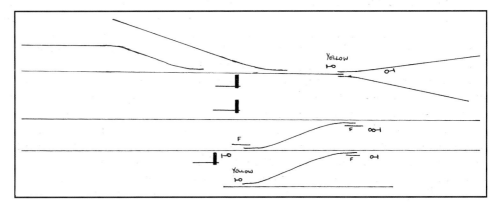

assembled signals available, designed to be built as operational models in 2, 4 and 7 mm scales. Scale Signal Supply, Model Signal Engineering in brass, wood and white metal, and Ratio in plastic are the three main sources who between them cover most likely companies and combinations of styles, periods and detail.

I am the first to admit to possessing not too much knowledge on signalling, and had envisaged a veritable forest on signals at Platt Lane. However, the photographs of the prototype, Great Moor Street, revealed surprisingly few. I am indebted to John Matthews, the LMS Society's signalling expert, for putting me right on the signalling needs for Platt Lane, and for emphasising, much to my surprise (and relief), that the railway companies did not generally, and the LNWR in particular, provide signals just for the sake of it. It was rather that the signalling was provided, as indeed was the track plan, for the use anticipated, which perhaps explains why it is often difficult to signal correctly model railways that don't owe their origins or operation to reality. A sketch is enclosed showing Platt Lane's signalling diagram, and a photograph showing the construction of a typical signal.

I haven't, you may note, discussed signal operation, but I find is generally best done with a solenoid: this is referred to in the first volume of this series, *Baseboard Basics and Making Tracks*.

Signal boxes

The signal box is a prominent feature on most model railways, and one that can be quite difficult to model effectively from scratch.

Signal boxes require a somewhat different approach to construction from other buildings. You might wonder why we should consider the building of our own signal boxes when there are a variety available in kit form - even in O gauge. Well, there are indeed some good examples on offer from the model trade, but they tend to represent a standard type produced by a particular company. Nothing wrong with that, you may think, but signal boxes used by railways come in a variety of styles and, while a company such as the LNWR did produce standard designs, they varied in size to suit their function at each specific location. Furthermore, style also varied, and standard designs were adapted to suit locations such as an over-track version.

As with signals, railways did not usually replace signal boxes for the sake of it, or just because they had a new standard design; consequently, even on the same route it is not uncommon to find variety in signal boxes. Until standard designs were adopted it was not unusual for railway companies to 'buy in' signal boxes from specialist signal contractors such as Saxby & Farmer; indeed some still survive in use today. There were also many standard designs acquired with the various railway amalgamations and acquisitions that were commonplace in early railway history.

There are a whole host of reasons, therefore, for treating the signal box like any other building and tailoring it to the site and its needs and functions rather than just saying 'Ah a Midland signal box - that will do nicely!'. While it is quite possible to adapt and modify the offerings from the trade, a range of much more interesting and rewarding possibilities

Here is a standard company signal box at Preston adapted to suit its unusual location; the entrance, toilet, etc, have been moved round to the back from the more usual gable end. There's plenty of interest in this shot - the ironwork of the canopy, the huts and point rodding, cranks and signal wire. *Eric Blakey collection/L&YR Society*

Thornton Ground Frame, near Cleveleys on the Fylde Coast, apart from being ideal for the smaller layout, oozes detail for the modeller. The ground signal (with a yellow rather than red stripe on the disc - see page 79) is interesting, being bolted to a concrete block. Note also the informal coal heap beyond the fence. *Eric Blakey collection/L&YR Society*

results from building your own, and I find it easier and no more time-consuming than starting to modify what someone else has designed and developed, good though it may be.

You need to assemble the appropriate information on your box before you can begin to model it accurately. There is much recorded information on signal boxes in the model press, as well a number of weighty tomes on the signalling practices of various companies - plenty of information, therefore, on common practices with dimensions or at least scale drawings. Furthermore, many of the 'standard' designs produced by railway companies were built in standard sections or bays, so even if your drawing is too big or too small and is of a standard box, you can easily enlarge or reduce it in the same manner as the railway companies did.

The basis for signal boxes is 20 thou plasticard, on which all the sides and ends are marked, a bit like 'cornflake packet' buildings. Openings for doors and windows are marked in pencil and cut out, after which the walls are cut. You don't, by the way, need to worry about window frames at this stage - it is only the openings for doors and windows with which we are concerned.

Each wall is now worked on individually, and the next stage is to build up the detail for the brick or stone walls. Embossed sheet is ideal and is added to the basic wall, but is cut so that the edges overlap the wall by $^1/_2$-1 mm at each edge. Clean up the openings before adding further details - the sketches on page 85 should explain this. Planked boxes require a slightly different approach from brick or stone-built boxes, and this is also shown in the sketches.

The walls are strengthened by gluing in 60 thou plasticard inner walls in the locking room (ground floor) up to floor level. Don't forget to cut holes for the windows and doors a good 5 mm bigger all round than the 'outside' openings, and to ensure that the inner wall is the same height all round - it forms the base for the floor. Similarly, don't forget to cut the inner wall short enough to fit inside the adjacent walls. When dry, check the fit and, using the inner wall as a guide, cut a further piece of 60 thou material for the floor - remembering of course that this fits inside, not on the ledge! - and a second for the base.

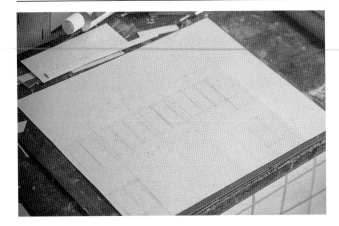

Signal boxes require a variation in building techniques to most other buildings and I have referred in detail to this in the text and included some sketches. Here the basic four walls of the Platt Lane signal box are being drawn out on 20 thou plasticard. In this case, rather than use embossed boarding the planking is being scribed. *All photos P. Smith/Kirtley Models*

Once the walls are drawn out, the planking scribed and the windows cut out, the sides and walls are cut from the sheet.

Each wall is assembled individually, and detail, doors and window frames, etc, are built up from plasticard strip. In this case glazing was added from 3 mm polystyrene sheet to give the model some strength. There is, after all, rather a lot of 'glass'.

As described in the text, the signal box walls are assembled around a floor of 60 thou plasticard, and because there is so much glass and the building is in a prominent foreground location, the interior walls are detailed, ie the planking is shown.

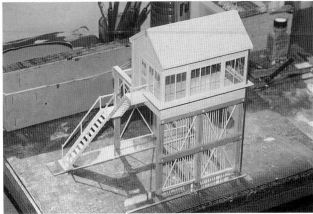

Signal boxes demand some attempt at interior detailing, and to achieve this I usually arrange for the roof to be made removable, as in this example, at least until the building is finally painted and detailed.

Platt Lane box is a standard LNWR wooden box but is unusual in that it is mounted on stilts, over the track. This, in the model, helps to disguise the entrance/exit to the fiddle yard immediately behind it by directing the eye - but is not out of keeping. The vertical rods are part of the linkage between the levers and the point rods and signal wires.

Assemble the walls, floor and base, fitting one end and one side together with the base and the other end wall with the floor, ensuring they are at 90 degrees.

If you are intending to model the interior of your box, you should consider at this stage the interior walls above floor level. Be it planking or brick, you will need to cut some embossed material or planking for the interior walls and fix this in place (perhaps only really a consideration in 7 mm scale or above). Paint the inside walls below floor level black, and when dry glue the two sub-assemblies together.

Doors and windows are next, and if you are lucky you may be able to find suitable etched windows. Otherwise it's out with the scalpel and 20 thou plasticard to cut your own. Be careful to incorporate any idiosyncrasies of design such as the Midland's 45-degree upper corners, and to get the windows to look as though they may slide - perhaps you could leave one partially open and a signalman leaning out?

When the windows are complete, the interior can be detailed. I believe at least a representation of an interior is called for, even in N gauge. Indeed, Springside produces an excellent set of castings with which to accomplish this task, with enough bits and pieces for all but the most fastidious.

Roofs are generally removable to allow access to the interior detail. The basis for all roofs, whatever type - and there are several - is a fake roof; generally 40 thou plasticard is good enough. The same basic process was described earlier for other buildings (see pages 62-63), but you may come across a hipped-roof box, as used by the GWR for example, a type that needs a slightly different approach as shown in the sketches.

The completed signal box on the layout with a finish typical of the period being modelled - unpainted for many years! *Author*

A closer view of the weathered box from the rear, showing detail of the supporting structure, door and windows. *Author*

A further close-up view giving a glimpse of the interior detailing. The weathering of the outside of the box was achieved by a wash together with dry brushing. Extensive use of grey has toned down the colours, giving the authentic forlorn look. *Author*

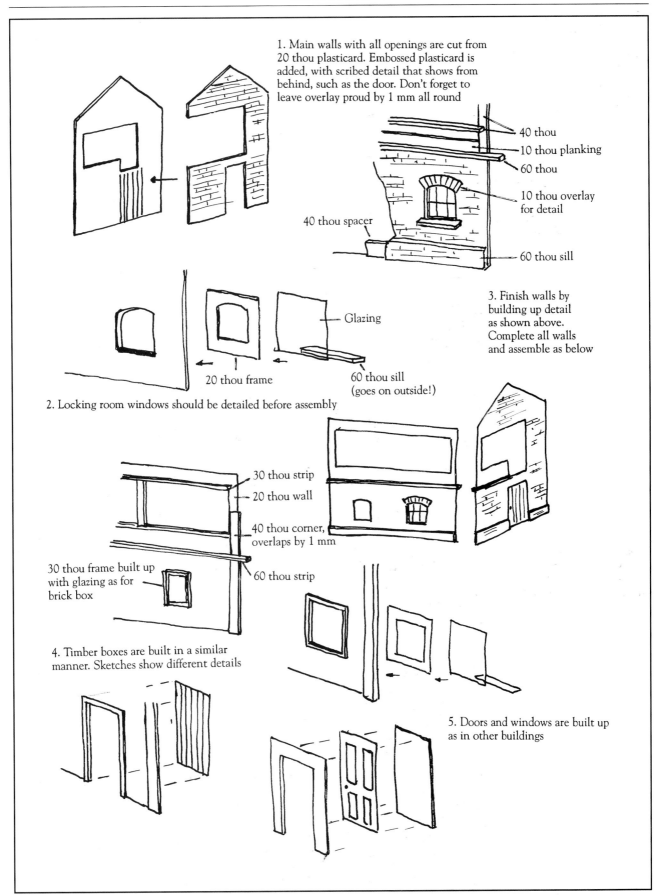

1. Main walls with all openings are cut from 20 thou plasticard. Embossed plasticard is added, with scribed detail that shows from behind, such as the door. Don't forget to leave overlay proud by 1 mm all round

40 thou

10 thou planking

60 thou

10 thou overlay for detail

40 thou spacer

60 thou sill

Glazing

3. Finish walls by building up detail as shown above. Complete all walls and assemble as below

20 thou frame

60 thou sill (goes on outside!)

2. Locking room windows should be detailed before assembly

30 thou strip

20 thou wall

40 thou corner, overlaps by 1 mm

30 thou frame built up with glazing as for brick box

60 thou strip

4. Timber boxes are built in a similar manner. Sketches show different details

5. Doors and windows are built up as in other buildings

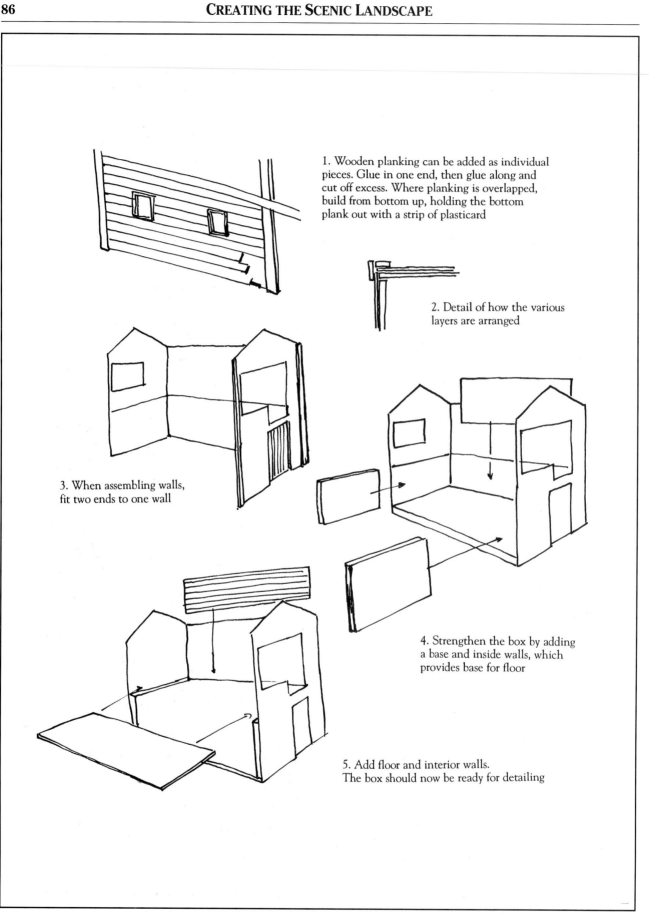

1. Wooden planking can be added as individual pieces. Glue in one end, then glue along and cut off excess. Where planking is overlapped, build from bottom up, holding the bottom plank out with a strip of plasticard

2. Detail of how the various layers are arranged

3. When assembling walls, fit two ends to one wall

4. Strengthen the box by adding a base and inside walls, which provides base for floor

5. Add floor and interior walls. The box should now be ready for detailing

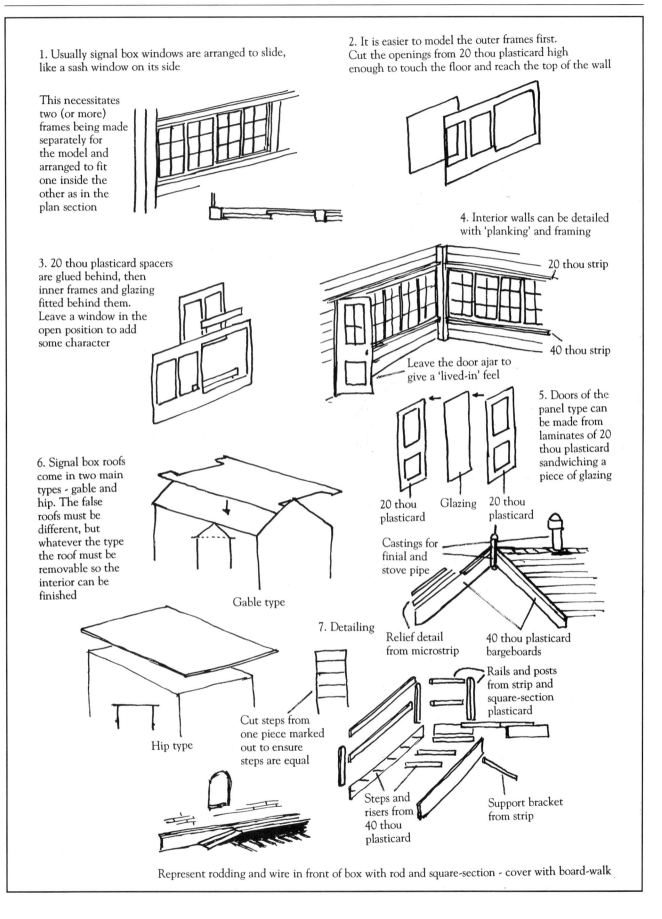

1. Usually signal box windows are arranged to slide, like a sash window on its side

This necessitates two (or more) frames being made separately for the model and arranged to fit one inside the other as in the plan section

2. It is easier to model the outer frames first. Cut the openings from 20 thou plasticard high enough to touch the floor and reach the top of the wall

3. 20 thou plasticard spacers are glued behind, then inner frames and glazing fitted behind them. Leave a window in the open position to add some character

4. Interior walls can be detailed with 'planking' and framing

20 thou strip

40 thou strip

Leave the door ajar to give a 'lived-in' feel

5. Doors of the panel type can be made from laminates of 20 thou plasticard sandwiching a piece of glazing

20 thou plasticard   Glazing   20 thou plasticard

6. Signal box roofs come in two main types - gable and hip. The false roofs must be different, but whatever the type the roof must be removable so the interior can be finished

Gable type

Hip type

Castings for finial and stove pipe

Relief detail from microstrip

40 thou plasticard bargeboards

7. Detailing

Cut steps from one piece marked out to ensure steps are equal

Rails and posts from strip and square-section plasticard

Steps and risers from 40 thou plasticard

Support bracket from strip

Represent rodding and wire in front of box with rod and square-section - cover with board-walk

5.
POPULATING THE LAYOUT

People and animals

Adding living creatures, human or animal, to a layout is essential, but perhaps you are wondering why it is worth raising in this volume. It is because it is often done as an afterthought with little care and certainly not the attention to detail and reality necessary to contribute to and complement our efforts in other areas to create a picture.

It is extremely difficult to give a realistic impression of animals and people because, unlike other aspects of the model, these animate objects must be modelled fixed to the spot. This, you may say, is equally true of road vehicles, and you would be right, but it is easy to overcome this by parking vehicles or showing them in a position in which no illusion of movement is necessary - for example loading and unloading, at a taxi rank or bus stop, broken down, or a farmer adjusting an implement behind his tractor in a field.

The same approach needs to be adopted with people and, to a lesser extent, animals. In practice this means avoiding placing them in a position where they are in an action pose but obviously not moving - a galloping horse or a running man, for example. Rather place them in positions where their lack of animation is not obvious and the pose not essentially one of action.

Take, for example, children playing football on a bit of wasteland, a very typical everyday scene. If they appear to be running around all over the place it becomes obvious after the first glance that they are in suspended animation. However, this is less obvious - but the scene you are trying to convey equally effective - if the children are standing around, the ball

Attention to the track at Bolton Shed in 1959 - much needed by the look of things - a commonplace activity in the period of our model. Move the man with the crowbar to stand outside the track 'talking' to the others examining the problem and you have a simple cameo for the model.
D. Hampson

The first view of '050 TE' tank loco No 508 being prepared at Boulogne shows how not to pose a figure on a model railway, as does the following shot of the *mécanicien* leaning out of the cab of '231E' 'Pacific' No 9 as it waits for the off with a Paris boat train.

However, pose him like the man in the third photo and, since it appears that he is doing something within the cab, it won't matter whether the loco is stationary or moving. Similarly, providing you have a spare loco to park beside your water crane, the pose of the footplateman in the fourth view would not look out of place and provides a little cameo on the layout. *Author's collection*

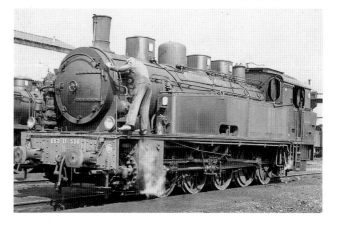

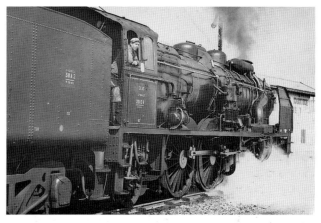

being 'spotted' for a penalty, the kicker standing in debate with team-mates and the goalkeeper standing anxiously awaiting the shot. In effect, we are masking the lack of movement by showing the scene where naturally there is little animation.

In the same way, standing groups of passengers talking on the platform or sitting reading the paper, and porters looking at the bags they are to carry rather than trying to show them walking or carrying is much more effective. I am not, however, saying that no movement should ever be indicated; rather that it should be done carefully to avoid the figures looking obviously out of place.

The next most important consideration with people is costume and painting. Increasingly in the larger scales there are some very detailed figures becoming available, well sculpted to give very realistic animals and people. Their quality demands careful use and painting, and their costume period, and what they are doing, for example soldier, businessman or labourer, is obvious at a glance. Careful painting brings them to life.

It is amazing the number of shining plastic figures still seen on model railways, stuck down as an afterthought; the least any modeller can do is ensure a matt finish and avoid vivid colours.

When it comes to animals, reference to the real thing is equally important. I watched carefully on one occasion as with obvious pride animals painted the previous night were planted on a layout prior to its exhibition, until a dark brown, bay horse appeared with a flaxen mane and tail. Well, unless it was a mutation you don't naturally get flaxen mane and tail with a dark bay horse. You don't have to know anything about livestock to know that it doesn't look right. Reference to the real thing or a book - colouring from what is natural rather than the imagination - would have avoided this. The quality of the white metal animals now available for O gauge is superb - a few blobs of black and white for a Friesian cow or grey for a sheep won't do, I'm afraid.

I have over the years come to the conclusion that railway modellers tend to be somewhat insular in their art, copying and learning from each other rather

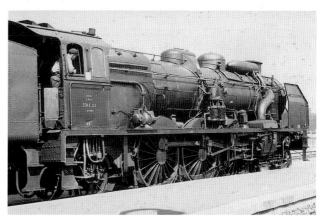

A group engaged in loading and unloading general merchandise from open goods wagons. Until the Second World War much more general goods were carried in open wagons than covered vans. *John Harmon*

An Edwardian platform scene with figures naturally not doing anything to portray movement - a good example from life that modellers would do well to copy. *Author's collection*

than looking around them. It is my belief that we can learn a great deal from other modelling disciplines and, in particular, military modellers, who can produce quite fantastic dioramas with unsurpassed detail, particularly in respect of people, animals and road vehicles. I feel we can learn much from military modellers, and a few hours spent looking at their work and examining their techniques would be time well spent.

Without, however, necessarily going to the lengths of our military modeller friends, but taking a few tips

from their practice, I have shown some examples of how the population of the layout can be painted. Perhaps the easiest and most significant improvement we can make in the use of livestock on our model railways is to paint them properly and put them down on the layout as they appear in reality, and not as we think they will behave. Next time you're out and about take a note of the disposition of sheep and cattle in fields and copy this on your model. By all means develop cameos - and I've enclosed a picture that would form an ideal one using a few cows, bushes and typical ramshackle fence. Forget the nice clean, tidy, sterilised image of the countryside - as many people find to their cost when they move to it, it's untidy, noisy and smelly. The majority of working farmyards are a haven of untidiness and a depository for broken machinery and materials that 'might come in handy one day'!

Little cameos dotted around a layout such as this add a little bit of life and character to the model. The carefully fitted and painted stone setts can be seen. *Author*

Typical disposition of cows! This is an ideal and easily reproduced scene for a cameo on the model, but note the ground condition and the colour of the fence - definitely not the black seen all too often on model railways, but faded grey/brown! *Author*

Careful painting of the excellent detail of cast figures is essential to bring out the full character of the person - buttonhole, buttons, moustache and beard, collar and tie are all clearly discernable. *Author*

War medals, dark glasses and white stick show a simple interpretation of a cast figure. Is the pint cause or effect? *Author*

Simple grouping of figures is necessary to achieve the best effect. As shown here and described in the text, avoid placing them in an 'action' pose. *Author*

Road vehicles

Road vehicles, motorised or horse-drawn, are an essential part of the scene in which the railway operates, and therefore we need to include them on our railway. We must, however, avoid their over-use, with our station car park looking like that of a supermarket on the last shopping day before Christmas! Moderation and understatement are the key.

These days for most countries, periods and scales it is seldom necessary to look beyond what is available from the trade; and what is not directly suitable can be modified or 'kit bashed'.

The railway companies themselves, from their earliest days through to the present, have always been great users of road vehicles, the earliest of course being horse-drawn, a practice that continued until well after the Second World War. The vast number of

The railway companies themselves made much use of horse-drawn vehicles, and fortunately a good many are preserved, particularly drays such as this GWR example on display at Oxenhope on the Keighley & Worth Valley Railway. *Author*

Horse-drawn vehicles were a common sight until shortly after the Second World War. They did continue, albeit decreasingly, for some years after the war, and here we see what is believed to be the last horse-drawn milk float in Bolton - in 1964! The photograph reveals the vehicle's conventional origins before it received its upperworks and roof. *D. Hampson*

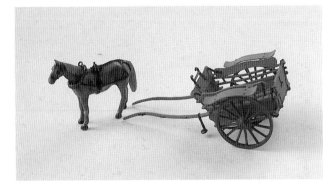

An example of a 7 mm scale white metal kit painted to represent a typical Sussex cart. Liveries at one time varied from area to area on the more simple country vehicles. *Author*

An example of a straightforward conversion by Mike Rush of the Widnes Model Railway Group from an inexpensive plastic kit to provide an authentic GWR road vehicle. *Author*

horses used required the employment of large numbers of people, the provision of stables at all but the smallest yards, the provision of provender stores (the GWR had a huge one at Didcot), and also provision for the horses' care and welfare. The GWR, for example, had a horse hospital, again I believe at Didcot.

The vehicles themselves came in all manner of sizes and types, from small two-wheeled carts to huge wagons drawn by two or more horses. The vehicles were often built in the railway companies' own works, although outside builders were also commissioned. Wheelwrights, blacksmiths, harness-makers and farriers were just some of the specialist trades employed.

It is commonly assumed that bus services were introduced as a result of competition from road services, whereas in fact many railway companies introduced their own omnibus services, the earlier

Right A readily available diecast car, but just a light weathering and the picking out of the windscreen wipers transforms it from a toy into an integral part of the Platt Lane scene. *Author*

horse-drawn vehicles usually mirroring contemporary practice of non-railway examples, incorporating open tops, outside staircases, etc.

The railways also developed other vehicles or adapted existing types to their own use, the Scammell 'mechanical horse' being a good example. Mobile road cranes were developed by the LMS for working at different locations and for maximum flexibility in yards. The Great War, or rather its aftermath, saw the major push to motor transport for the very simple reason that a large number of military-surplus vehicles became available which railway companies were

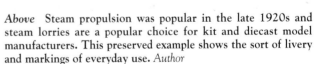

Above Steam propulsion was popular in the late 1920s and steam lorries are a popular choice for kit and diecast model manufacturers. This preserved example shows the sort of livery and markings of everyday use. *Author*

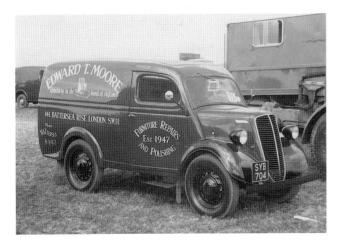

Above A light delivery van of the early post-war era with typical lettering displaying proud ownership and use. *Author*

Right One of several different body styles that were fitted on the 1940s Bedford chassis, a versatile vehicle for any model railway. *Author*

BR, like its predecessors, was a great user of road vehicles. Here are two typical examples of common vehicles from the 1950s and '60s, a Scammell 'mechanical horse' and trailer and a parcels van - note the poster on the van's side. *Eric Blakey collection/L&YR Society*

encouraged to buy. Many were adapted for railway use following their purchase, often being fitted with the company's own specialist bodies. There were many British truck manufacturers in the inter-war period - AEC, Thorneycroft, Morris, Bedford, Austin to name the most common - and there was considerable joint development of vehicles between these manufacturers and the railways, for example cattle wagons, tippers and parcel vans. The railway companies also developed joint cartage and omnibus services.

Agricultural tractors were widely used as a basis for hauling trailers. Contract hire schemes with major companies were developed whereby vans were hired out for the exclusive use of the hirer; Cadburys, McFarlane-Lang and Rowntrees were amongst the companies taking part.

The year 1927 saw the introduction of pneumatic tyres, vehicles prior to that having solid tyres. The 1930s saw the development of the mechanical tractor and trailer arrangement, while 1934 saw the patenting of the Scammell patent coupling which, when adopted by the 'Big Four' railway companies as the standard, guaranteed wide introduction of the Scammell 'mechanical horse', firmly established as part of the railway scene until the decimation of the general goods services in the 1960s.

One often overlooked aspect of the onslaught of road vehicles is that, like the horses, they required places for storage and service, and this resulted in the construction of local garages, often only big enough to hold, say, one bus. Road vehicles were seen by railway publicity departments as an ideal mobile advertising

Most of the 'fleet' users of the period in which Platt Lane is set took a pride in their vehicles, and while it is necessary with vehicles as with figures to place them carefully on the layout, it would as a rule be wrong to resort to major weathering. *Author*

hoarding, and from the earliest days not only did railway-owned vehicles proudly display their owner's services, but also its posters advertising services such as freight cartage and the lure of holiday destinations served by the trains.

Clearly, road vehicles were and indeed still are an important part of the totality of the model railway scene. The period, owning company, area and traffic type on your model railway should determine what you employ. Once again, above all don't overdo it - take a good look at photographs of the area and period you are modelling and try to establish some feel of what was actually there. Remember that the private car was until the 1950s far less common than commercial vehicles. Avoid obvious traps, and don't just put a vehicle on the railway because you like it - a cattle wagon in a coal yard won't be very helpful in creating a good overall impression.

There are, thank goodness, a great many commercially available vehicles available in scales which, if not exactly those in which we are modelling, are sufficiently close to be pressed into service. I am thinking here of the many 1/50 scale diecasts that can find a home on O gauge layouts.

If you resort to kits, there are a vast array of products covering cars and commercial vehicles of all periods, from relatively inexpensive plastic kits to quite expensive £40ish metal ones. Military vehicle kits provide, particularly for the 4 mm scale modeller, a good source of parts and a choice to adapt and modify the components from their intended use. If many of these are not of British type, they are often sufficiently similar to be of use. I have enclosed a photograph of a model converted by Mike Rush of Widnes Model Railway Club from an inexpensive plastic kit, and one showing how diecasts can be 'improved' to help them blend in with the rest of the layout. Basically, effective use of road vehicles, horse-drawn or otherwise, requires observation, a bit of discipline in choice and disposition, and a bit of thought and care in appearance - in essence, the same approach that I have suggested is followed all through, from design to construction and operation.

Road vehicles do provide an opportunity to develop cameo scenes on the layout, which hold the attention and break up visually the mass of the layout. But as always they need to be understated rather than leap out at the viewer and deflect from the overall impression.

The type of thing that springs to mind is, for the 1950s for example, an AA Land-Rover parked in front of a car, patrolman and driver looking into the open bonnet, an array of tools (adapted from a footplateman's oilcan, spanners, etc) on the floor with perhaps a petrol can or a dark patch on the road to represent the escaping oil. I don't think I would go so far as the fitting of a small smoke unit to the car to represent the steam from an overheating radiator though. . .

A lorry loading or unloading; a horse-drawn delivery cart with the horse having its nosebag and children looking on; a man standing in the road backing a vehicle into a factory entrance - man waving, driver leaning from the window - the possibilities are endless.

In conclusion, for all the perception about vehicles in the correct period, there is always some anachronism that upsets the order we like to put on developments. Take a look at the accompanying picture of the milk delivery cart - the caption explains.

In conclusion

In drawing this volume to a close, I am conscious that I have tried to cover a wide area and that I may be guilty of stating the obvious to some and missing out bits which I may think obvious but others may not. Such is the difficulty of trying to strike the best balance!

It is my sincere hope that you will have enjoyed this book and, more importantly, that it has encouraged you to have a go and in doing so take a closer look at the real thing, contemporary or historical, urban or rural, to develop your ideas and modelling. It is my belief that there is no secret to successful modelling beyond patience and the application of careful observation. If asked for a single phrase to sum up this philosophy, I would say 'forget the slide rule and rely on the eye'.

The next volume in the series looks at the construction of the locomotives and rolling-stock in detail and, perhaps more importantly, why certain locomotives and vehicles were chosen, how train formations were compiled for the services we needed to run, and their operation. I hope that if you have enjoyed the story so far you will join me for the next instalment.

INDEX